God
can
be
trusted

Other books by Martin and Elizabeth Goldsmith
Getting There From Here
Islam and Christian Witness
What About Other Faiths?
What In The World is God Doing?

God
can
be
trusted

Elizabeth Goldsmith

OM
publishing

Second edition 1984
Reprinted 1989, 1990, 1993

This edition 1996
Reprinted 2000

OM Publishing is an imprint of Paternoster Publishing,
PO Box 300, Carlisle, Cumbria CA3 0QS, UK
and PO Box 1047, Waynesboro, GA 30830-2047, USA
http://www.paternoster-publishing.com

02   01   00   7   6   5   4   3   2

British Library Cataloguing in Publication Data
A catalogue record for this book in available from the British Library

ISBN 1-85078-243-1

Printed in Great Britain by Cox & Wyman Ltd., Reading

Contents

Preface

A small group of people had gathered around my husband and myself at the end of a meeting. One of them, an athletic-looking young man over six foot tall, leant forward and picked up a book from our bookstall.

'I've seen this one before!' he exclaimed, leafing through *God Can Be Trusted*. His eyes were shining as he looked at me. 'I was based in the Namibian desert for a time, and someone lent me a copy. It was a tremendous encouragement to me when I was in a particularly lonely situation.'

I felt deeply humbled at the privilege of being able to help someone like this. From time to time we have met others: a couple working in the United Arab Emirates told us how their faith had been restored through reading my life story; it had steadied the resolve of a nurse working in war-torn Afghanistan in an incredibly difficult situation; and a housewife living only a few miles from my home in Hertfordshire shared with me that she had become a Christian through reading my book.

And so it is with a deep sense of privilege and gratitude to God that I write a preface for this fifth impression of *God Can Be Trusted*. In the 1984 impression I added an extra chapter, bringing the story up to date. Today I am again challenged to look back and see how God in His love has always been caring for me and leading me, even when times were particularly dark.

In recent years, as a wife and mother, I have come to see more clearly the deep hurt which I felt as a child being separated from my parents for five years because of the Japanese war in China, and losing my mother during that time. Very lovingly, God has brought me to a healing of those memories.

'Where was God?' I could be asking, as I see myself once more, a lonely six-year-old, left by my parents in the headmistress's study of a boarding school in north China. More deeply than ever now, I know that He was with me.

There are many today who carry pains and scars from the past. If I had not known deprivation, I would be less able to understand their needs. And it is my prayer that my experiences may move many to thank God for any difficulties in their lives, and to be grateful for what suffering can teach us. God can bring good out of the worst hardships. Our difficulties may provide the raw material for His miracles.

As this new impression goes out, I pray it will not only encourage others to commit themselves fully to the God who can be trusted, but also that it will challenge some to serve the church of God in some of the countries mentioned. After forty years of Communist rule in China, we see today the miracle of a church which has survived years of ferocious persecution and grown out of all recognition. China's doors are gradually opening for foreign Christians to become resident there once more. And much can be done to build up national Christians.

Malaysian Christians today face severe government opposition, and any witness to the Malays may bring imprisonment. While it is impossible now to enter this country on a missionary visa, doors are wide open for those with secular professions or business connections to serve the national church.

Indonesia, with her huge churches, now offers only limited openings for missionary personnel, and higher qualifications are often required. But once inside the country, there are enormous opportunities to minister to the fast-growing churches who are hungry for Bible teaching. In each of these countries the church is vibrant and strong. The potential is great as they begin to catch the vision of playing their part in world-wide mission.

May God call us all to a deeper trust in Him, and a greater commitment to sharing his saving love with the whole world.

Elizabeth Goldsmith
All Nations Christian College,
Hertfordshire,
England
January 1989

Foreword

I TURNED TO the young mother; 'How can you be sure that God will look after you and your children if you go overseas as a missionary?'

Her eyes held mine confidently as she replied, 'Since I've been at All Nations and got to know Elizabeth Goldsmith, I've come to see that without any doubt God can look after me in just the same way that he looked after her!'

God has entrusted Elizabeth with experiences that are out of the usual, although I didn't know that when I first heard about her twenty-five years ago. She and my fiancé (now my husband) were students and worked together on the committee serving the London University Christian Unions. I remembered him speaking of this student wistfully – it seemed that the calibre of her faith and certainty in God were rare indeed.

We followed her movements after she left university, joined the Overseas Missionary Fellowship, and went to Indonesia as a missionary. She didn't disappear from sight like many of our contemporaries, for a steady flow of writings began to come from her pen.

Because I knew of Elizabeth, I was interested in her and started to read anything she wrote. And from her pen came stories based on her experiences that encouraged and strengthened me enormously.

Before long, John and I followed her overseas with OMF – to a different part of South-East Asia. But Elizabeth's writings continued to help me. I wanted to believe that God would look after our family, and that I could trust him to do so – but I knew that if he failed and we had made a mistake then we'd be in the soup and it might be too late to put things right. When I doubted God, then at the right times writings like Elizabeth's came my way.

The sharing of her experiences gave me the courage to take a step into the dark and to see whether God could be relied on in the different situations I faced as a new missionary. Would the God who helped Elizabeth really help me too? Her testimony played a significant part in my daring to live and work in OMF – a missionary society that does not appeal for funds, and trusts God to meet needs in answer to prayer. I found I could rely on God as she did, and incredibly he worked things out beautifully for me.

This book is one that has been significant in my life. Through it I have been privileged to share in God's dealings in Elizabeth's life and family, and the ways in which he has provided for them even when things seemed pretty impossible.

'God can be trusted' is the message of this book. It is a message that we need to grasp in an era in which we tend to trust the welfare state, and to forget that God is perfectly able to meet all our needs. The fact that God can be trusted to work things out to fit in with his overall and long-term plans for us, for others and for different places and situations, is something that we need to grasp in an era when Christianity tends to be shallow, immediate and more man-centred than God-orientated.

This book gives God the pre-eminent place and puts man where he should be, in second place. But it will deepen your realisation of how much God really does love individuals and the extent of his care and concern for you.

Anne Townsend

Chapter One

Internment Camp

THE ROAR OF an American B.29 grew steadily louder over our internment camp. We children could contain our excitement no longer.

'Please let us go out and watch,' we begged, bouncing up and down on the top of our trunks, which served as our only chairs.

The teacher hesitated a moment. A new hope was forcing itself into her tired eyes. The atmosphere was electrifying. Doors were banging all over the crowded old building. The noise of running feet and excited shouts came from outside.

'All right, we'll break up the class,' she said. Before the words were out of her mouth we were off, jostling and pushing one another to reach the door.

What a sight met our eyes! The huge American plane, now certain of our position, had just swept back over our heads, leaving a trail of tiny specks behind. One of the specks suddenly puffed out as if an invisible hand had just inflated an enormous golden balloon. Then another did the same . . . and another . . . scarlet, turquoise, emerald and peacock blue, the parachutes began to float down.

'Parachutes!' Everyone was shouting it now. My eyes grew big with wonder. Living in far-off China, I had never seen an aeroplane before, let alone parachutes. And what was that swinging underneath them? Two tiny black legs silhouetted against the deep blue sky. They were men! These were paratroopers! Might we be free at last?

Every able-bodied person in our camp was out of doors at that moment. And now the swelling crowd began to surge down the main street, past the low rows of houses and on towards the gate. Hardly noticing where we were going, we children were swept along too. The startled Japanese guards stood with fixed bayonets beside the gateway. They had seen the parachutes dropping. Rumours must surely have told them that World War II was nearly at an end, but they had received no order from their officer, and uncertainty made them hesitate. Their choice of action was taken out of their hands, as like a tidal wave the crowd swept on past them and out through the gates. With a helpless gesture the guards lowered their bayonets and stood aside.

To be free! For a moment the reason why we were all running was forgotten, as I suddenly realised I was outside those towering grey walls. I was in a field. The scent of new-mown hay reached my nostrils. A wild flower was blossoming at my feet. I could go where I liked and no one was stopping me! The expanse of blue sky had never seemed so wide above me as it did on that day.

Shouts brought me back to the immediate situation. A crowd was gathering round a tough lanky American. His first reaction on rolling to a stop had been to unhitch his parachute and immediately draw his pistol. He had not known how strong the Japanese troops were in this area, and expected to fight his way through to our gates. But here he was being given a hero's welcome by a near-hysterical crowd of raggedly-dressed prisoners. Women threw their arms round him and kissed him. The men tried to grasp his hands or slap him on the back. Finally they lifted him shoulder-high and carried him back to the camp.

The field was now filled with a mass of excited people, running in all directions. Some were laughing, some were crying. Many hugged each other. Others could be seen stumbling along the path, their faces streaming with tears of joy. Some of us bare-footed children raced over to the little stream which bounded the meadow. We splashed and whooped and waded in the water in utterly abandoned joy. Our scanty clothes were soaked in a few moments, but we did not care. We were deliriously happy. We were free.

The mob of laughing, jostling internees carried their rescuers on their shoulders back to the gates of the camp. In their elation they were oblivious to the fact that the American soldiers, their arms at the ready, were watching for any hostile move on the part of the Japanese guards. For a moment tension rose as the Japanese had to decide whether to fire at point-blank range on the newcomers. For the second time in a bare half-hour their reactions appeared overruled by some invisible force. Instead of firing they saluted; and the crowd surged forward again.

Perhaps the most dramatic moment came when the American major in charge leapt to the ground just inside the gates and demanded to be shown the office of the Camp Commandant. The crowd watched in awed silence as the tall major carefully checked both his service pistols and, with a high sense of the dramatic, strode through the office door with both pistols at the ready. The Commandant could not possibly have had time to consult his superiors in Tsingtao in the short interval since the plane had wheeled over our camp. If his side had already surrendered, it would go badly for him if he now killed this army major; yet if all were not over, it would mean utter disgrace to hand over his fifty well-armed soldiers to a mere seven paratroopers.

For the third time a split-second decision had to be made. Tensely the two leaders eyed each other, every muscle on the alert. Then slowly the Japanese Commandant reached for his samurai sword and gun, and handed them over.

Among the seven paratroopers, there was one who had specially asked to be allowed to join the mission. He had been a pupil at the very school I was attending — the Chefoo School.

We bombarded him with questions, 'Why did you come by parachute, and all so suddenly?'

'I guess you guys didn't realise,' he drawled in reply. 'Up in those hills are two Chinese guerilla bands. We had news that as soon as peace was signed they were planning to capture your camp. You would have been valuable hostages and they are short of cash. So we reckoned we just had to get moving! Actually our plane took off two hours before the Peace Treaty was due to be signed,' he glanced at his watch, 'but it should be settled by now. It sure is good to see you Chefoo kids. Where's Mr. Bruce, the headmaster? I remember him well.'

The Chefoo School had been founded for the children of missionaries of the China Inland Mission. It was situated right beside the glorious North China coastline. A beach of golden sand lay just over the road from our main entrance. Bamboo-covered hills sheltered it from behind. I started there in 1939 just as World War II was beginning, but as the fighting was far away my first two years were peaceful.

My father held the post of medical superintendent of a large mission hospital a thousand miles away to the far north-west. With aching hearts our parents had had to leave their six children at the mission school. They believed God had called them to share their faith in Him with the Chinese people. They knew too that if the education of their children were not to suffer we must be separated from them for a while. Being myself a missionary mother now, I know it was a desperately difficult decision for them.

The Japanese never reached the part of China where my parents worked, but soon after Pearl Harbour we felt them closing in on us at Chefoo. The teachers sheltered us younger children from the suspense which they were daily facing. All we knew was their apparent conviction that, however things worked out, God would still be in control.

One day Japanese troops marched into the town. Our headmaster, Mr. Bruce, together with five other leading westerners, was imprisoned for several weeks for interrogation. Everyone was ordered to wear arm-bands and we were forbidden to leave the school grounds. I walked sadly round the small cement play area of the prep. school thinking, 'I wish I could scramble over the rocks again, hunting for sea shells. I wonder if we shall ever walk along that pretty stream again to the Bamboo Temple. What fun it would be if we could clamber over the hills once more to Castle Rock!'

Gradually four of the six men who had been kept for questioning were set free, but Mr. Bruce and one other were still being held. Every day during school assembly we prayed for these two, and the staff must often have prayed as they went

14

around their ordinary work. They had no one who could help them except the God in whom they believed. We were all enemy personnel, living on conquered Chinese soil: we had no right to expect mercy at the hands of our victors. With a half-formed belief, we children watched to see what would happen. Was the God who claimed to work such miracles in the Bible still alive? Did He really exist? And if He existed, did He really care?

Many people today would not agree with the way I was brought up. They might feel that our missionary parents and teachers were indoctrinating us. What right had they to force their beliefs on our childish credulity? Yet all parents are planting some kind of belief in their children; their way of life can demonstrate that there is a God who cares, or that religion is irrelevant. Through the testings of Japanese captivity we had an unusual opportunity to see if our teachers' faith was realistic.

After several more weeks of waiting, our headmaster was released, considerably thinner, but otherwise none the worse for his ordeal. His companion was never heard of again.

A short time later the school was seething with rumours. That morning Japanese soldiers had been round to all the foreign business people in the town of Chefoo. The peremptory order was given, 'Vacate your homes by twelve noon and be ready to move to other premises.' With only three hours in which to sort through their belongings and make arrangements for the future, they faced a nearly impossible task.

As a school we waited in suspense. Would the same command come to us? The Japanese could so easily want our lovely buildings — a fully equipped compound with a boys' school, a girls' school, a preparatory school, together with a spacious sanatorium for convalescent missionaries, and numerous smaller houses for the staff.

Hastily a suitcase was packed for each child. But nothing happened. One week went by, then two. Finally word came from the Japanese commanding officer: we were to vacate our buildings, as he required them for a military hospital, but we were being given a whole week's notice, and forty lorries would be placed at our disposal to help move our belongings! One of the teachers remarked, 'We don't know the future, but how wonderfully God looks after the details for us!'

When we learned where we were going, the prospects did not appear so encouraging. The whole school was to be crowded into a few private houses at the other end of the town. It sounded a physical impossibility — groups of sixty to seventy people squashed into each family-sized house. How would we ever fit in? What about all our stuff?

The day came, and with it the convoy of lorries. We all assembled in the entrance hall, each child carrying a small bag of his own possessions. Our sense of excitement was slowly being swamped by uncertainty and fears. The fully-armed Japanese guards, lined up with military precision by the gates, did nothing to allay our anxiety. We must have looked a woebegone sight as we began to file out of the buildings.

Then away to the front someone struck up a song:

> God is still on the throne
> And He will remember His own . . .

The words were picked up along the line. We caught them and joined in too:

> Though trials may press us
> And burdens distress us,
> He never will leave us alone.

Our childish trebles merged with the deep bass of the older boys and the masters. With gathering confidence and heads held high, the whole school caught the melody and began to sing:

> God is still on the throne
> And He will remember His own.
> His promise is true, He will not forget you,
> God is still on the throne.

Past the startled soldiers we marched, and out into the busy Chinese street.

We slept like sardines in our new home. School work was done sitting on the mattresses on which we slept. There was nowhere to play, few books to read, and food was short. Lying awake the first night, I heard the distant toot of a car. It was a melancholy sound and aroused an intangible home-sickness. When would we be free again?

Ten months dragged by under these crowded conditions. They passed like a sort of nightmare — an empty, in-between stage, where we belonged nowhere. I felt all the time that it must be a bad dream, but somehow I never managed to wake up.

Yet day by day the teachers would have something fresh for which to praise God. Someone had smuggled in several packets of seeds, and the older boys were being organised to plant out a vegetable garden. Piglets had been acquired; maybe if they were fattened up, they would help out our meat allowance. One day we were all settled down with pen and paper to write to our parents — a German family in town had undertaken to post the letters in small country letter-boxes. They trusted that if only a few were mailed at a time, they might get through.

At last we were told that we were to be moved to a much bigger internment camp for all the enemy civilians in our area of North China. It meant another upheaval, but rumours had it that there would be room to move about and play, and to gain the mental stimulus of meeting other people. For our teachers it meant the chance of sharing with others their responsibility for so many children's lives.

Packing was not so easy this time. Our journey was to start with three days at sea in a small Chinese vessel. Our few possessions were tooth-combed again, so that only the essentials were taken with us. The rest was to be sent overland – we hoped! On arrival we were actually without beds and mattresses for two weeks until they caught up with us. Fortunately we had not known this beforehand.

Everything we owned was sorted through radically.

'Please let me take my big doll,' one girl begged.

17

'No, only the little one,' the teacher said. 'You won't be able to carry them both, and I can't make room for them in the suitcases this time.'

'But I must take my teddy bear,' I burst out, clutching my beloved one-eyed treasure.

Seeing the look of anguish in my eyes, she relented. 'All right. I'll tie a piece of string on him and you may hang him round your neck. You'll need both your hands for carrying your cases.'

That evening we climbed up the gangway of the little ship, wondering how the whole school would ever pack in. We girls were crammed into the darkness of the hold with hardly space in which to stretch out. Some were already beginning to feel sea-sick as the ship rolled in the choppy bay. A little girl began to cry with fright at the darkness and the strange smells. But our teachers were facing a bigger problem: the food which they had ordered for the journey had not come. A few small packages had been delivered to the ship, but the bread on which they were counting had not arrived. Holding hands in the unlit gloom we all prayed together, asking God to send us the food we needed. As if to mock us, we heard the ship's engines starting. The rumble of the anchor being pulled up drowned our voices. A steady throbbing seemed to shake us through and through: we realised we were slipping away from the harbour with very little food for our three days' journey.

Hugging my teddy tightly I tried to forget the pangs of hunger and settle down to sleep. I felt too bewildered to cry, too insecure even to know how to express it. Was God still on the throne?

I had scarcely fallen into a restless slumber when shouts awoke me. 'The bread's come! The bread's come!' Was I dreaming? No. Someone pushed a chunky piece into my sleepy hand. The scent of its oven-fresh sweetness woke me up. As I lay happily munching I heard what had happened. For some reason the ship had been delayed again after sailing. Our enterprising Chinese baker, noticing what had happened, hired a launch and chugged after us with his precious load. He just had time to swing it on board and receive his payment before we set out again. We could none of us believe this to be mere chance or coincidence: we felt it was God himself lovingly caring for us and answering our prayer.

The Chinese vessel we were sailing on was hopelessly over-loaded. If there had been a storm we should hardly have stood a chance. But apart from a strong swell which upset some with more delicate stomachs, all was well and we arrived safely at Tsingtao. From here we were taken forty miles by train and lorry, standing crowded together like animals in a cattle-truck, until we reached the internment camp at Weihsien.

To our dismay we soon discovered that conditions were no less crowded here. 1,400 people were herded together into this American Presbyterian mission compound measuring only 200 yards by 150. But at least the overall space was greater than our previous quarters, and there was a softball field where games could be played.

We gazed at our new environment with curiosity. The mission station had been built to house a hospital and Bible college. There were a chapel and various large buildings for lectures, as well as rows and rows of single rooms where the Bible students had slept and studied. Into these rooms, measuring about seven feet by nine, a family of four had to squeeze themselves. The unmarrieds were crowded into the lecture-rooms which served as large dormitories. The camp authorities (all internees themselves) did their best to vacate a few rooms for our school, but this accommodation was scattered in various places, making it very difficult for classes to take place or for us all to get together for prayers.

The best accommodation in camp was the hospital — a well-designed modern building which was both warmer in winter and cooler in summer. This happened to be the only building tall enough to overlook the high walls which ran all around the compound. From there one could see the flat Chinese farmland and two small villages several miles away. When two men managed to escape and join the guerillas in the hills not far from us, the Japanese thought they must have been signalling from the top floor of the hospital. As a reprisal they moved out all the people who had been housed there and replaced them with our school. In future, only children were to live there. The staff were exuberant! Now, at last, we could function as a school again. What we had been powerless to alter, God had arranged for us.

Life in an internment camp left much to be desired, yet it is surprising how quickly one can adjust to even the most uncongenial surroundings. The Japanese guards left us to manage our own internal affairs and the leading internees organised the camp justly and well.

Such food as came in was cooked in two large kitchens, one catering for 800 people and the other for 600. The meat sent in was tough and almost inedible; probably it was donkey flesh. Such things as milk, eggs and sugar were almost unknown luxuries, carefully hoarded for expectant mothers or the diet kitchen. Every morning after the Japanese roll-call we would race down to the dining-room. Each clutching his own tin mug and plate, we jostled to glimpse the day's menu. Why we hurried I was never quite sure, as it was almost always the same:

Breakfast: Millet porridge, black tea, bread.
Dinner: Curry or stew, black tea, bread.
Tea: Soup, black tea, bread (and cake, if we were lucky!)

But perhaps today might be different. Usually the only variation came by ringing the changes between curry or stew. This was actually the same dish anyway, with or without the addition of curry powder. The evening's soup nearly always turned out to be what was kept back from the stew, watered down to make it go further. The more enterprising of the cooks occasionally baked what we all gallantly termed 'cake', made from local sultanas, flour and peanut oil. It made a welcome change.

I can remember walking through the grounds with one of our teachers, being taught which weeds were edible because we were desperately short of green vegetables. But what I hated most was being made to eat a teaspoonful of powdered eggshells every day to make up for the milk we were not getting. How we loathed the flat, dry, choking taste!

20

Six months before the end of the war, yeast became unobtainable, so the camp bakery was unable to produce bread. Considering how largely bread featured in our diet, this meant we were drawing near starvation point. I still have with me a childish diary kept for some months over that time. Day after day it reads, 'Still no bread'. There was no other entry: there really was nothing much else to say.

I suppose our teachers prayed about it as they did about every difficulty. I don't remember praying about it myself, but I do remember realising that my eleventh birthday was not far off and wishing that there might just be something special to eat on that day. Red Cross parcels should have been received by every member of our camp at the rate of one a month. The Japanese, however, saw to it that they never reached their destination: never, except for this once.

A few days before my birthday, word was flashed around that a train of donkeys carrying Red Cross parcels had just been let through the gates. The day before my birthday the parcels were distributed: coffee, butter, chocolate, jam, tins of salmon and peaches, milk powder and breakfast cereals — some of the contents we had almost forgotten existed. Our eyes were shining with joy as each child received part of the fabulous gift, while the teachers stowed the rest carefully away to be meted out gradually over the coming months.

So it was that on my birthday morning there were small parcels to be opened: two sweets from this friend, a packet of salted nuts from that, while my special boy-friend, Kenneth, had melted down his bar of chocolate and moulded it into a heart shape, studded with some of his precious currants. I had never seen anything so beautiful in all my life!

Cleanliness was a problem, as soap was desperately short. We were meant to receive one bar per person per month of the poorest quality scouring soap, and this had to last for the washing of all our clothes and bed linen, as well as for our own toilet. There was a large laundry in the basement of the hospital where sheets and towels could be scrubbed. It got to be quite a joke if people were running short of soap: if our school was running out of supplies, more soap would be sure to come into the camp! It happened three times — just when the school had been specially praying about it.

I disliked that laundry intensely. We were all supposed to help in what ways we could and since we prep-school girls were considered too young to wash and scrub, to us fell the lot of hanging everything out to dry. The winters were bitterly cold in that part of North China and I can remember even now how blue with cold my fingers would look as we struggled to stretch the flapping white sheets out over the drying-lines. The snow-laden wind would tug at the linen making it beat like the wings of a huge white bird, and after it had been out for some hours, it would gradually set hard and solid like an enormous sheet of ice, so that bringing it in in the evening was even worse.

Summer had its drawbacks too — hundreds of tiny flat-bodied red ones in the form of bed-bugs. However hard we fought to exterminate them, the few surviving ones managed to multiply so rapidly that their numbers were soon back to normal again. Quite unfairly, they seemed to be particularly fond of me. My legs and arms became a mass of bites where I had scratched at them in the night.

'Can you remember any vivid detail about camp life?' I asked one of my ex-teachers when I started to write this book. She looked at me with a twinkle in her eyes. 'Yes,' she said, 'there was my nightly routine before getting into bed.' Thinking it must be something to do with a regulation set by the Japanese, I looked at her, puzzled. 'Every night in the summer,' she continued, 'I'd go over to where you were fast asleep. You'd lie sprawled across your sheet, soaked with perspiration and wearing as little as possible. My job would be to pick off all the bed-bugs I could find.'

Chapter Two

Reunion

WHILE THE PARACHUTES were floating down over our internment camp my elderly father was hard at work in far Northwest China. During his ten-minute break from the operating theatre he was listening to the radio. The other young doctor and two western nurses leant forward eagerly to catch the words. It was true at last! The Japanese Commander-in-Chief had surrendered to the Allied Forces. All his troops were commanded to hand over their weapons. City after city in China was now being freed.

'How near to your children do you think our forces are now, Dr. Hoyte?' asked one of the nurses excitedly.

Father tried to control the emotion in his voice, 'It's difficult to tell how long it would take them to reach Weihsien,' he began slowly, 'and whether they are considered a top priority or not.'

'They could be there already,' broke in the other nurse. 'Just think, Dr. Hoyte, your children might be free right now.'

'Right now?' said father, hardly daring to believe it. 'Pray God they are still safe.' And he abruptly got to his feet and strode back to the operating theatre. How could he concentrate on the next patient when his mind was so full of other things? He put on his surgical overall and started to scrub up again; but his thoughts tugged him back. The children. There had been no news from us for nearly a year. Were we still alive? Dear Robin, the eldest, so gentle and confiding . . . What a wrench it had been to leave him at boarding-school for the first time . . . how Grace had felt it! Darling Grace — he could see her white face now and pleading eyes . . .

'Are you ready to begin?' The voice of the anaesthetist brought him back with a jump.

'Yes, yes, quite ready,' and he started to swab the incision area. But Grace's face came back. It struggled for predominance while father's fingers automatically continued their precise task. 'My children's mother.' His heart missed a beat. 'Why, oh why had they been so desperately short of vaccine? Why had it been Grace who had come home one evening with flushed cheeks and dilated pupils?' Typhus! By the next morning he had known what she was helplessly grappling with. But he had had to go back to the hospital: outpatients, ward rounds, administration . . . and then home late in the evening to nurse Grace all night. Desperately. Sponging her every half-hour to get the temperature down. Moistening her lips. How cracked and dry they had become! He had watched her in anguish, knowing that if it had not been for the war she would have been safely inoculated and would never have caught this terrible disease.

And then Grace had gone . . .

His fingers stopped their work, jolted into inactivity as the torrent of thoughts abruptly ended.

'Has his blood pressure dropped?' asked the nurse anxiously, wondering why father paused.

With a jolt he came back to the theatre, and mutely shook his head. He forced himself to go on, but his thoughts kept racing. They had been awful days: night after night of bombing; daybreak bringing crowds of wounded sufferers to the hospital. He had always made Grace go to the air-raid shelter when the sirens went. One of them must be safe to look after the children when the war was over. And then it had been Grace who had been taken . . .

How everyone had loved her — especially the leprosy patients, the very patients he could do nothing for now. He had no medicine with which to treat them. The only solution was to isolate them. But they had loved Grace! They begged to be allowed to come to her funeral . . . The far side of the chapel was where they had cordoned off an area for them. And the leprosy patients planted her garden with flowers — bright little dwarf marigolds, so gay and undaunted, so like Grace . . .

The air-raids had been terrible, a rabble madly rushing for shelter, the crush, the noise, the stench in the underground trenches. The ghastly aftermath, mutilated bodies carried in one after the other — to him, the surgeon. He must do what he could. Do what I can . . . Do what I can . . . But it's only a drop in the bucket. The sea of human misery swirls on and on. Will it never end?

But now, today, the news. The war ended. My children. I must get to them. I must find them. I must know if they are still alive . . .

At last the day's work wore to an end, and Father was free to hurry into the city before the Mandarin's office closed. He begged for permission to leave and travel to the coast. Two weeks of frequent visits had to pass before the reluctant consent was given. He had been scathingly reminded that the country was still in chaos, roads and bridges were bombed, and transport was impossible to find. He had had to promise that the younger doctor would take over all his responsibilities and the hospital would suffer in no way if he left.

And yet the question remained: how could he get to the coast? Our internment camp lay 1,000 miles almost due east across a maze of demolished roads and wild stretches of no-man's-land. His only hope was to head south for 500 miles to the great city of Chungking, which had served as the war-time capital, and from there to find a way of crossing the 1,000 miles to the sea. Even during the fighting a bus service had functioned fitfully along this Chungking road, and with the fighting ended there were hundreds of people who wished to use it. The officials told him he would have to wait a month or more before he could book a seat; and even if he set out, there would be no guarantee that he would arrive at his destination. Daily the missionaries met for prayer about every detail of the situation . . . and then left it all in God's hands. There was nothing else they could do.

Father packed as if his plans were all completed, went through the details of the hospital administration with the young doctor, and said his farewells to his Chinese friends. The day after he had finished, a messenger came running, and said,

'Quick, there is a seat for you in the bus which leaves at noon.' And so he began his eventful journey.

The bus was crammed to capacity with excited Chinese. Each one wore a thickly-padded gown to keep out the biting winds of North China. Bundles of bedding and the other luggage were swung up on the roof. Toddlers clung to their mothers as the bus lurched round corners, and Father squeezed into a narrow space beside them. His legs were so much longer than theirs that he could not sit straight. He crouched with knees turned sideways to avoid the passenger in front, and hands gripping the wooden seat so as not to bump his bald head against the low roof with every unexpected jolt.

Cold, cramped and stiff they travelled on day after day. The nights were spent in any wayside Chinese inn they could find. Father stretched out on his bedding roll on the heated brick *kang* beside the others, while the fleas enjoyed the unexpected taste of Western flesh! The food served to the travellers was of the coarsest — a bowl of noodles and vegetable broth morning and evening. At times there were rumours of brigands, and the driver would not travel that day; or a bridge was down and they had to make a wide detour to cross the river. Another time the driver lost his way through the hilly country.

After two weeks of such travel Father was aching in every muscle. And then they came to a wide river whose bridge had been washed away by floods; there was no other way across. Numbly the passengers tumbled out, glad to stretch their limbs for a moment. The children excitedly ran off towards the water but were angrily called back. One or two nursing mothers unbuttoned their gowns to let their babies suckle. The rest squatted stoically on the grass verge.

Father walked a hundred yards back up the road, enjoying the exercise, and then returned to join the others. After a long wait he went over to the driver.

'What do you propose to do?' he asked.

'Nothing,' the man grunted in reply.

'But you can't just squat there for ever!' Father expostulated. Another grunt was the only answer. Father turned helplessly to look at the other passengers, but they all appeared as inscru-

26

table as the driver. 'Well, at least I can get some exercise,' thought Father, and he walked back and forth a couple of times.

The hours ticked by and all he could do was pray. He knew that as the evening approached they would all have to turn round again and find somewhere for the night. Probably if the bridge were not mended the driver would find passengers who wanted to go in some other direction and would leave them all stranded at the tiny village inn.

'O God, what can I do?' he asked. 'Unless you send a miracle, I'm really stuck.'

Father believed in a God of miracles. Not that he expected to be picked up out of every bit of trouble like a spoilt child watched over by a doting mother, but he believed God Himself had led him to take this bus to Chungking. However many obstacles might come in the way, God would see him through. And so it worked out. As evening drew on, three American lorries rumbled round the corner and drove on past the group of staring Chinese passengers right up to the river's edge. Father watched halfheartedly to see what they would do. He expected they would turn round and drive off after a few minutes. Then to his surprise he saw two American soldiers wading into the water. He watched. They were up to their knees now . . . their thighs . . . they were carrying something which trailed in the water. It looked like a long piece of rope. Everyone was watching them now. They were waist-deep and sometimes missing their footing, but they struggled on. Then they seemed to get taller — they would make it across. The water grew shallower. The men clambered out on the other side.

Father jumped to his feet and went over to the officer. 'What are you doing?' he asked. 'Can you get across?'

'Sure thing,' the officer drawled, surprised to see a Westerner among the passengers. 'See this great winch on the front of our truck? Those two guys over there will haul the steel cable over to the end of that rope they're carrying. When they've secured it to that great tree we'll be able to winch ourselves across . . . Easy as anything,' he added, seeing Father's look of incredulity.

Father hesitated. 'I don't suppose I could come with you?' he asked. 'I know it would be a great favour and I hardly like to ask. But I'm trying to get to the coast. I must find my six children, they've been prisoners of war in Japanese hands for three years . . .' He broke off helplessly.

'Sure, we'll make room for you,' the officer smiled. 'It will be a bit crowded. But it won't be as bad as travelling on that old bus. Say, how far have you come on it?' And that was how Father drove in comfort in the cab of an American army truck into the great city of Chungking.

The long, jagged coast of China still lay 1,000 miles to the east of him, but he hoped that communications would be much better from there. Much to his dismay he found the city seething with ill-disciplined soldiers, penniless refugees and anxious merchants, all of whom were trying desperately to contact long-lost families or to get to some other part of China. He was curtly informed that there was no means of going to the coast except by plane, and that these were reserved for military personnel only. Baffled and weary, he knocked on the door of our missionary society's home in Chungking. They were well used to unexpected guests and he was warmly welcomed. A bed was found for him, but he could not sleep. He had been so excited at the prospect of seeing his children again. Now the weeks were dragging by and still he was no nearer the coast. Where were his children, anyway? Could he be sure he would ever see us again? God had taken his wife — had He taken his children too? Would he arrive at our internment camp only to find the Japanese had shot us all? Morning came and with it the struggle for consciousness, the struggle to come to grips with his situation, smothered by the yearning to sleep and sleep. It was all too hard, too many obstacles in the way. He felt dazed, aching with tiredness in every limb.

The household gathered for a simple breakfast. It was difficult to join in the dining-room chatter when all the time his heart was a thousand miles away. His missionary friends understood his silence and made no attempt to intrude. Each one had been through years of stress and could sympathise in the deepest way. They gave him all the help they could offer — food, shelter, help and advice, and above all their prayers.

When the offices re-opened the next day Father went into the city to explore every avenue he could to obtain transport to the coast. He had been given several contacts and these led to others, but they all drew the same response:

'I'm sorry, the railway lines have all been blown up.'

'No, there are no roads open to the coast.'

'The planes are completely full with military personnel.'

The situation appeared hopeless. It seemed he would have to wait for months until normal communications were established. Then one day somebody asked him, 'Did you know that the Red Cross are looking for doctors to care for the prisoners of war in the Shanghai camps?' Might this be the opening which he was looking for and which would provide him with a way to reach the coast? He hurried over to the Red Cross head-quarters.

'Yes, we are urgently in need of doctors,' the official behind the counter replied, 'and we are willing to take on any qualified personnel, no matter how temporarily ... We have planes at our disposal. We could fly you to Shanghai if you would promise to work for the Red Cross. But as soon as you receive news of your children you may relinquish the post.' It sounded too good to be true. A miracle had happened again.

Resplendent in the uniform of a Red Cross doctor, Father flew the next day the remaining 1,000 miles to Shanghai. The passengers all sat on their luggage as the transport plane held no seats. The heating-system was out of order, which made the flight perishingly cold. But that did not matter; he was on the next lap of his journey and would surely soon link up with his children.

If he could have seen us at that moment Father would have been amazed. We were seated in the expensive dining-room of the exclusive Edgewater Hotel in Tsingtao, a well-known holiday resort. I was desperately trying to keep a stiffly starched table napkin on my knees. It helped to hide the fact that the dress I was wearing was two years too short for me. My knife cut joyfully into a luscious pork chop. Immaculately dressed waiters whisked the empty plates from us, replacing them by even more delicious courses, while we made ourselves ill with the delights of eating. Our whole school had been brought to Tsingtao by train as the internment camp disbanded and we spent a fairy-tale week there.

Looking back I can only remember it as some dreamland fantasy: sleeping on a real bed at last, swimming in the hotel's private pool, and wandering with unaccustomed freedom through the wooded headland to gaze over the vast expanse of sea. As we watched the water proudly crash on the dark rocks and then sweep off again into the depths of the ocean, we knew that we too were free to go anywhere — everywhere. I was young; I could run and shout and sing; yes, life was good.

Father caught up with us a month later in Hong Kong. We had been taken there to await a ship home to England. After endless enquiries he at last found out where we were. Thankfully he relinquished his commission with the Red Cross and hitch-hiked down to Hong Kong on a naval sloop.

One of the teachers called out to me, 'Elizabeth, your father has come. He's over by the Reception Office.'

With pounding heart I ran to find him, one awful fear tugging at my consciousness. Would I recognise him? I had been only six when I had last seen him. Would I hurt him now by not knowing him and run past him looking, looking?

And then I was in his arms, the strong arms of the half-familiar stranger who was my father, and we began the gentle, probing process of getting to know each other again.

Chapter Three

England

WE ARRIVED IN England one cold December morning just before Christmas 1945. Our troop-ship was crammed with returning prisoners of war. We slept in lines of swinging hammocks over the long tables on which we ate our meals. Few of us owned more than the clothes we stood up in, though when we arrived in Aden the British Red Cross officials attempted to make sure that everyone had at least one warm jumper or a coat. By the time our family reached the head of the queue they had run out of clothing and I came away baffled with three skeins of bright pink wool in my hands. What could an eleven year old do with these? I didn't even possess knitting needles!

England increased my sense of bewilderment. The train from Southampton drew in at Waterloo station and then we walked *down* a long flight of steps to arrive at street level. Had the train been flying? It had appeared to me to be running on terra firma!

My father's sister kindly took us two girls to live with her temporarily, while his brother took him and the four boys. Everything was strange to me in this new English home. The chairs in the lounge were so comfortably upholstered they looked like thrones to me. I was amazed to see my aunt sit down on one. The dining-table was polished so highly I hardly dared touch my fork for fear of making a scratch, and when after lunch I was given the brush and crumb tray and told to sweep the crumbs up on the table, I stared at the brush and burst into tears. How could I touch that beautiful table — the only thing I'd ever swept had been the floor!

Father, thankfully settling his boys into his brother's household, faced much bigger problems. At sixty years of age he had no home, no wife, no job, and six children to educate and care for. Someone remarked that he reminded them of the veteran trooper pacing Trafalgar Square with the placard:

Battles	4
Wounds	5
Children	7
Total	16!

When other men were thinking of retirement, Father was forced to start life afresh. He resigned from the missionary society which he had served for thirty-two years, in order to make a home for all of us. Finding work was not easy. Although he was a well-qualified doctor and surgeon, infrequent visits to England meant that his medical knowledge had not kept pace with recent advances. Who would be willing to employ him as a doctor at his age?

Next to Father's need to find work was his need to make a home for us all. After the war there was a desperate shortage of houses in England. And where would the money to buy a house come from? Life as a missionary had not made it possible for him to store up large savings. If he found a house, how could we manage to run it? My sister Mary and I did not know the first thing about housekeeping. We all needed a mother. Yet would anyone dare take on six step-children?

As the weeks went by Father was able to see that the God he had trusted as a young man was not going to let him down now in his old age. Friends were wonderful in turning out their wardrobes and finding clothes to fit us all. We did not care that it was second-hand clothing; it all felt new to us. The four of us younger ones were able to get into schools and the two oldest into colleges, and to our relief we found we were able to hold our own with others of our own age, for right through the years of the war the staff of Chefoo School had continued teaching us as if we had all been in our own premises. As each July came around they set their own matriculation examinations, based on the standards of the Oxford Overseas Examining Board. When the pupils had written their papers, these were all placed in envelopes and sealed, to be kept safely until the end of the war. Oxford University agreed to mark the papers and through this means my three oldest brothers gained their matriculation.

What thrilled me at going to an English school was that I was given a crisp new notebook for every different subject. I felt a sense of almost holy joy each time I wrote on a new clean page. In camp I owned one notebook for the whole of the three years. I wrote in it very lightly in pencil; and when the end was reached, rubbed it all out carefully and started from the beginning again. Now as I turned over a new page I felt the same exhilaration one feels when stepping out into an untrodden field of sparkling snow.

Perhaps our greatest need as a family was for a mother.

Up three miles of narrow country lanes from Barnstaple in north Devon stood a lovely old country house. Eileen Drake and her sister Madge were running it as a guest-house, looking after their elderly parents at the same time. They had known Father before he had gone to China, and now Eileen wrote to invite us all to stay over Easter. She first met my father when she was little more than my age and he had been a medical student. But then he left for China and married, and she had hardly seen him since. Within a few days of us all arriving Father asked her if she would marry him. It must have seemed like a bombshell to her, and looking back now I cannot help but admire her courage. She said yes, and they were married within three months.

Meanwhile other exciting new developments were taking place. Father found a job. He was appointed principal of a small college in north-east London which offered a year's course in medicine to out-going missionaries. There were enough rooms in the rambling old building for our family to live there as well, and by August we were all united again.

For everyone in England the post-war days were difficult, but my step-mother seemed to have more than her fair share of worries, trying to start a home for us and to win the affection of her six step-children. After our war-time experiences we children were happy to live anywhere, but our new mother surveyed the house with dismay. Troops billeted in it for the last three years had left it in a terrible state: doors had been forced open and were now lacking both locks and handles; broken windows swung from insecure hinges and rubbish was strewn everywhere. What had been the gracious home of a wealthy family was now a chaotic mess. A fiery-tempered cook and a dishonest charwoman added to Mother's problems. 'Oh, I wouldn't steal from *you*, ma'am,' one of them expostulated to her one day, when six pounds of our precious rationed sugar was found to be missing.

Father had his headaches too, with all the lecturing for thirty or forty students, when he had never done anything of this sort before. He loved teaching, but lecture preparation took up a tremendous amount of time, especially thinking how to put complex medical facts in a way which lay people could understand. The administration of the college was his responsibility too: correspondence with intending students, arranging visits to neighbouring hospitals and clinics, and supervising the repairs of the building. A further blow fell when, as a result of all that we had been through, my eldest brother had a mental breakdown and had to go into hospital for two years.

They were strange days; yet through it all I knew my parents were doggedly clinging to their God. Their circumstances tested them almost beyond endurance, but it was their faith which gave them strength to pull together and to pull us all through.

I had been watching their reactions as if I were an outsider. This God they knew, I wanted to love Him too: but He did not feel *real* to me as He did to them. After all, I could not *see* Him or *touch* Him. There was no answer I could hear when I prayed. How could I be sure that God really existed? Might not the happenings my parents attributed to Him just be due to mere chance? As I looked back, life had not all been plain sailing. If God was really there and loved us, why did He not stop wars? Why had He allowed Mother to die? Why had we as a family faced so many upheavals?

I felt very unsure of myself in my early teens and was quick to be on the defensive. So often I would be caught out over

34

some silly little thing which everyone else appeared to know except me. One of the clues for a treasure hunt at a friend's birthday party stated 'Near the settee'. What was a settee? I was far too shy to ask, too proud to say I did not know. It ruined the whole party for me.

After a year as a family together we went to Frinton for a holiday. Here a group of students and young professional people organised a children's holiday mission. My step-mother was asked to cater for the large houseparty, while we youngsters could join in with the games and other activities.

Each morning the team of workers went down to the seafront and gathered together any children and young people who wanted to join in. A varied programme of games, hikes and competitions was laid on, together with Christian services held right there on the beach.

It was during that holiday that one day Mother asked me point blank if I was a Christian.

'I don't know,' I said rather miserably. 'In some ways I want to be, but somehow it doesn't seem very *real*.'

'That's the thing about the Christian life,' she said, 'you've got to take it on trust.'

'But how can you trust something you can't see?' I said helplessly. 'I can love you and Father because I can see you. You're here. I know it. But God isn't like that. He seems so far away; and I never know if I've got through to Him. How can I possibly trust him?'

'It's a funny thing,' she replied, 'but all day long you are trusting things you can't see.' I looked at her surprised. 'What do you do when you go into a dark room at night time?' she went on.

'Well, put the light on, so I can see, of course.'

'Can you see the electricity?' she asked. I shook my head. 'Only you trust it don't you? Because you know it works. You know that last time you put the switch down the light came on. *Every* time you do it, it happens. So you don't think anything about it. You just trust that the electricity is there even though you can't see it. And even if the light *doesn't* come on you don't say, "that proves there's no electricity." You say, "the bulb must have gone — or the fuse — I'll ask Father to mend it." Faith isn't a difficult thing. Faith is something we are using all the time, only we don't think about it. When you post a letter, you have faith in the post office that they will see to it for you, and deliver it to the right address. When you get on a train you have faith in the driver: that he's *there* (although you probably haven't bothered to look) and that he knows where he's going and is able to take you there. And it's just the same with God. You can't see Him, but you can see what He *does*. You can see how He has looked after us as a family and answered our prayers. He wants you to trust Him, just like you would trust the train driver. Step on to God's train — His will for your life — and say you are willing for Him to guide your life and take over completely.'

'But you can *say* these things, Mother, and still not feel any different afterwards,' I said, still doubtful.

She smiled kindly. 'This is where you must just take His promise and trust Him. Let's look and see what He has said.' She opened her Bible and read, ' "As many as received Him, to them He gave the right to become the sons of God, even to them that believed in His name." What does that last bit tell us we have to do?'

'Believe on His name.'

'What is His name?'

'Well, Jesus.'

'Yes, and Jesus means Saviour. He wants you to believe that He is your own personal Saviour, that He came to this world to die not just for everyone, but for you, Elizabeth, and that because He has died you are no longer guilty before God. You are forgiven. You can now know God as your Friend. He will guide you and help you all your life. You'll get to know Him better and better as you share everything with Him and one day you will go and live with Him for ever. And what does the first bit of the verse say?' Mother went on.

'As many as received Him,' I read out.

'That's the other thing you have to do. Not only believe Him, but *receive* Him. Ask Him to come into your life and make it His own. You may not feel any different, but you have His promise. And here you've got to trust Him just as you trust the train driver. If you believe Him and receive Him, He does something you can't see and makes you into a child of God.'

'Can I do it right now, Mother, because I do want it?' I asked.

Together we prayed, and I told God in very simple words that I did trust Him and I wanted to receive Him: please would He make me His own child.

I did not feel any different after that conversation except that something had been settled once and for all, and now I was to find out just what it involved. I certainly did not lose my diffidence, or change in any radical way outwardly. I was just as selfish as before and would bury myself in some Baroness Orczy thriller, not noticing the mound of housework which Mother had to get through. Yet deep down there was a change. I knew I belonged to God. If He wanted to do something in me or through me I was open for whatever it was.

Chapter Four

A Home – at last

THERE IS A promise in the Bible which means a great deal to those who take God at His word: 'Those who honour Me, I will honour.' For me as a teenager, as I watched what happened to my parents, I saw this promise come alive.

Father had told us how three times during his years in China he lost all his possessions and had to set up home again from scratch. How I loved to curl up on the shabby old couch in our living-room and hear him tell of some of his adventures. When he left us all at Chefoo school, it had taken him and Mother three months of dangerous travel before they reached the hospital in far-off Lanchow. The Yellow River had flooded that summer, spreading its waters over hundreds of miles of flat farm-land and carving a complete new watercourse for itself. As the waters receded, large uncharted lakes were left behind, some of them twenty miles across. The small party of four missionaries had to cross the waterways at four different times.

One night in a hired Chinese boat they were being rowed over the dark swirling water. Suddenly there was a crash of splintering wood. They all lurched forward. Their boat had collided with a partially submerged tree trunk, and water began pouring in.

'We're sinking! We're sinking!' the excited boatmen cried.

'Quick, row us over to that sandbank there,' Father called out, indicating a dark shape not far away. The 'sandbank' turned out to be the remains of a peasant home which had collapsed in the floods, turning into a soggy heap of straw, sticks and mud. Hastily the luggage was tumbled out of the sinking boat and piled up precariously on the tiny island. The missionaries and boatmen scrambled on top of the unsteady edifice, clinging on to whatever they could. There was so little room that only Mother was able to sit down; the rest stood or crouched, holding on to any projection, and watched their boat sinking ominously into the darkness. One final surge of sucking water momentarily marked the spot where it disappeared. Cramped and stiff, they waited as the hours dragged past. Eventually by the early light of the next morning they were able to hail another passing boat.

The floods formed a sort of no-man's-land between the invading Japanese forces and Chinese guerilla troops. At a later stage the party was fired on three times by soldiers and narrowly missed being hit. One guerilla chief refused to allow them to proceed through his territory for several days. During his enforced wait Father began treating some of the soldiers for minor ailments. Among them was the chief cook who had a badly ulcerated leg. Afterwards the cook put in a word for them, and a few hours later boats appeared to take them on the next part of their journey.

They were almost through to the next mission station and were spending the night in another guerilla camp, when one of the party noticed two strange well-roped bundles among their luggage. His suspicions were aroused.

'What are these?' he asked the coolies, and when no one would reply he insisted that the parcels be opened. Inside were forty-eight packets of heroin! To be caught with such a drug on one's hands could mean immediate imprisonment, and possible death. Father insisted that the bundles be removed at once. One of the coolies, very frightened, stammered out, 'Those don't belong to us; they belong to Mr. X,' mentioning the name of a plump-looking Chinese merchant who had been tagging along with their party for the last few days.

'Well, call him to remove them,' Father retorted.

'I can't. He won't be back until the evening,' was the frightened reply.

'Make sure when he does come that he removes them at once! Permission may come for us to travel again tomorrow and we can't leave this inn with that stuff in our possession. The soldiers might search us.'

Next morning the coolie assured Father that the heroin had been disposed of. But as no sign of Mr. X had been seen, Father ordered a search through the luggage. Sure enough, one by one all forty-eight packets were found hidden in the bedding-rolls and among the cooking-utensils!

Just then a soldier stepped through the courtyard gates. 'You have the guerilla chief's permission to go,' he announced. 'Pack up your things and leave at once.'

The missionary party stared at each other in consternation. What should they do? If the packets were left behind they would be discovered and the ownership traced to *them*.

The soldier became impatient, 'Get moving,' he shouted at the coolies. Each one bundled luggage on to their rough wheel-barrows and the front ones began to move off. Miraculously, when only three carts were left, Mr. X appeared. The heroin was forced unceremoniously into his hands, and the party made off, leaving him standing alone in the empty courtyard with the incriminating goods in his possession!

When visitors called, we also loved to produce Father's medals.

'Tell them about this one,' I would urge, holding up a large heavy star suspended by a wide navy and scarlet ribbon.

'Oh, that one was given for fighting the plague. See, I've written the translation here. 1916. I must have been in China only three years at that time.'

'The plague?' our visitor would question. 'You mean, like the Great Plague of London, and all that?'

'Yes, it came sweeping into China across the Great Wall from the north. It must have originated somewhere in Mongolia. City after city was decimated as the infection spread. The Government called for doctors to volunteer and stem the tide. Although my language was still poor, I had just been put in charge of a small hospital in Linfen. So we closed that temporarily, feeling that the need in the north was far more urgent. Two Chinese Christians volunteered to go with me.'

'But how did you fight it? Was there some sort of inoculation

41

you could give? Weren't you frightened of getting it your-selves?'

'No, we had no inoculation. The main thing was to isolate the sick people and prevent others from getting bitten. You see, the infection is carried by fleas. They normally live in rats which are the common scourge of the countryside there. When the rat dies, the fleas hop away to find some other flesh to live on. Whoever they alight on will come down with the plague. It was as if doctors were spread out in a thin line right across the front of the oncoming wave.

'Our first problem was that no mandarin would lose face by admitting that the plague had come to *his* beautiful city. "We're quite clean!" they would say. "Oh yes, there's plague in the countryside, but not *here*." And then you would go out and see corpses rotting in the street!'

'However would you tackle such a situation?' someone would burst in.

'We would dress up completely in overalls, boots, gloves and masks. We couldn't afford even one flea-bite! And then we went to any houses where we were told someone had died. I remember the others would never dare go inside; so I always had to lead the way. Once they saw me go in, they would follow. Of course, we couldn't touch the bodies, so we used grappling hooks to lift them on to the stretchers and carry them out. The essential thing was to bury them deep enough so that no fleas could hop out, and no rat could get in.'

'You really ought to write these stories down, Dr. Hoyte,' somebody once exclaimed.

He looked up mildly surprised. 'I never thought there was anything wonderful in them. This sort of thing was happening to missionaries all the time.'

Life, following the will of God as he saw it, had certainly taken Father into many difficult situations. It would have been much easier to set up a comfortable medical practice in Eng-land. But 'Those who honour Me, I will honour' was God's promise. And it really worked.

Father had lost so much in China, but God knew how to

make it up to him. Now after some years living in the dilapidated medical college for missionaries, God gave us an even better home. I say 'God gave us', because we could not have obtained it for ourselves, and it came as a specific answer to prayer. The college where we had lived stood in a dingy part of the East End of London. Our new home was to be in Chislehurst, Kent — an expensive residential area, with a beautiful bracken and silver-birch common right opposite our front door. The college had fallen into such a bad state of repair that one of us, pushing his chair back from the dining-room table, made a hole right through the floor and narrowly escaped crashing through into the glass-encased museum of awful tropical diseases which was housed immediately below! Workmen discovered that the whole of our dining-room floor was riddled with dry rot and had to be completely replaced. But our new home was a lovely house built by the inventors of Chubb locks, who really knew how to build things to last.

So we moved to Chislehurst, where my parents were to be wardens of this hostel for medical students intending to become missionaries. The students lived in this delightful green belt area, travelling up to London every day for their studies. Since my elder brothers were now away at college, only my sister Mary and I lived at home. Mary was to start her training as a radiographer at the Middlesex hospital, London, and this again seemed to us all such an answer to prayer. My parents could not afford to pay the £200 for her course, but a friend whom Mother had greatly helped several years before offered to pay it all.

I had been used to cycling to school with Mary every day, and now had to face a new school on my own. It brought back all the old diffidence and fears. I should not know where to go or what to do. What if I made a mistake? But I was older now and learning to cope with things to some extent in my own way. I would screw myself up and nothing *would* go wrong. I would watch, and make sure, and never be caught out. I would study hard. No one would beat me at the top of the class. I *could* do it. I would show them all. And I did. I'm a perfectionist at heart, so I set my standards high and drove myself. I loved

43

study and knowledge for its own sake — and for the challenge of mastering as much of it as I could. I used to bury myself in books, and be lost in a far-away academic world where people did not matter; mere facts and information were all that counted.

Educational methods have changed radically in the last twenty years. I was never really taught to *think*. It was easy to sit there smugly at the top of the class, amassing knowledge of every kind, but completely missing the whole point of the world around me, which was *people*. And underneath there was still the lack of self-confidence, the fear of standing up in public to say anything, the inability to lead others or to maintain discipline as a prefect, because I had never learnt to come to terms with myself.

We all have our teenage romances; for me it was with one of the medical students. He was tall, fair-haired and full of fun — just what any girl would dream of. He had us all in fits of laughter describing a hitch-hiking holiday he had taken all the way up to the Cairngorms, and the next moment he would melt my heart with the description of holding a fragile newborn baby moments after it had struggled into this world. But he did not care for me; and one day he told Mother why. He said I was hard. It shattered me. Was I really? Was it something I had said or done to him? I knew it wasn't that. It was the basic *me* underneath, and the shell I was building up around myself. And so he slipped away. Later he became engaged and then married. Of course I told myself he was far too old for me. But that did not affect the basic hurt. I knew what he said was true. I hated the things I saw inside myself, but I was powerless to change them.

It is fortunate for us that God has a place in His scheme of things for even the most unlikeable people. Some of us would be dropped like a hot poker if He hadn't!

One afternoon I came into Mother's darkened room with a tea-tray. She had been in bed all day with a bad migraine.

'Draw the curtains back a little,' she said. 'I'm feeling a bit better now. A cup of tea would be lovely.'

I gave the soft blue curtains a little tug, letting in the

slanting rays of the warm afternoon sun. The breeze from the garden was heavy with the scent of roses. I watched it for a moment gently tossing the long branches of the graceful silver birch which stood on the edge of the lawn.

'Tell me how school went today,' Mother said. Perched on the end of her bed, while she poured herself out a cup of tea, I shared with her some of the day's happenings.

'Do you know what I was thinking about while lying in the dark?' Mother asked after a while. 'I was reading last night about India and the terrible things they used to do before Christianity came to that country. Some Indians were willing to do literally *anything* in order to find peace of heart. Sometimes they would hold their arms above them as if in prayer for day after day and week after week, until they lost all ability to move them: they were stuck above their heads for ever, shrunken and small from lack of use. Others would kneel in prayer and only crawl about from place to place on their knees, until they became quite incapable of ever straightening their legs again. All because they longed for their sins to be forgiven, and were desperate to earn forgiveness at any cost.'

'But that's *awful* when you think that Jesus has done everything for us,' I burst out.

'Yes, but they don't know,' went on Mother. 'They don't know that Jesus has borne all the suffering that was necessary and there is nothing that we need go through to earn forgiveness. But there was even worse than that. In South India there was a huge idol called the Juggernaut. Normally it stayed in its great temple behind massive doors. Once a year they lifted it on to an enormous cart and dragged it through the town at the centre of a great procession. There would be music and dancing and chanting crowds. Everyone would be out on the streets that day to watch. And one or two who found life too great a burden — who longed for peace of heart — would fling themselves under the wheels of the Juggernaut and be crushed to death.'

There was silence in the quiet bedroom. What could one say in the face of such utter despair?

A few moments later I went to my own room, took out my

45

little diary and wrote there, 'Mummy told me today about the Juggernaut in India. And God told me He wanted me to be a missionary.' It had come to me as clearly as that. If there were people in the world so desperate, it was my job to share with them the good news I had.

I started being a missionary in a small way at school. It took a good deal of courage to knock on the headmistress's door and ask if I could start a Christian Union. Our Head had always appeared to me rather frightening — small, but neat and trim, with short grey hair. She moved with an air that commanded respect, certain of where she was going and what she was doing — the very opposite of stiff and diffident me!

My suggestion was rather coldly received. It was not that she was against Christian things, but she obviously did not want some religiously fanatical schoolgirls stirring up trouble by thrusting their own exaggerated ideas down other people's throats. I stood there, quaking, on the deep pile of her carpet, listening to her lecture on Christianity not just being singing and prayers, but involving the whole person. I must take care to pull my weight socially and on the sporting field — in fact, not develop into a lop-sided personality.

However, eventually the suggestion was accepted. For my last two years we had a flourishing Christian Union held in the science laboratory after school hours, to which thirty or forty girls would turn up. With my parents' wide circle of friends it was not difficult to find visiting speakers. I was terrified of standing up in front of such a large group of girls to introduce the speaker. But fortunately only a few words need be said and I could thankfully sink on to my chair again and leave the rest in expert hands.

Eventually the committee who were in charge of our hostel for medical students decided to move the hostel up to London and my parents felt they should give up the job. For one thing they did not fancy a return to rows of tall houses and dingy streets, and for another they had had enough of working for committees and wanted to branch out on their own.

But what should they do? We had been in England seven years now and Father was not getting any younger; neither was

46

my step-mother. Because of living abroad, Father had not paid sufficient contributions to draw his old-age pension, and even if he had, he still had three children dependent on him. A pension would not go far among five people.

And then an idea came to them — to buy a house in the country and run it as an old people's home.

Under our Welfare State, almost every age group seemed to be well cared for except the old. Such homes as there were tended to be large, impersonal institutions, where there was not time to give individual care and attention. Mother, who had had a great deal of experience in running a guest house during the war, felt she could cope with the organisation of such a home, and having a retired doctor on the premises would be a great draw.

The problem was the finance. Where should we find enough money to buy a house sufficiently large to hold both the elderly people and ourselves? Through money inherited from his father, Father had been able to save £3,000. £1,000 he had invested in England, £1,000 in America and £1,000 in China. The money in China was a complete write-off; he eventually received 13/4d in compensation for it! That left him with £2,000, and by selling his life insurance he was able to make it up to £3,000. We children had also been left money — a further £3,000 — which was added to the pool. £6,000 would not go far towards buying and fully furnishing a house of the size we needed.

My parents prayed constantly about it. This was no quick and easy 'Please God, show us what to do, Amen', but a real waiting in God's presence. They prayed and then paused for God to put His thoughts into their minds. They prayed again, thinking through every possibility which came up.

But it all drew a blank, while the deadline for us to move came nearer and nearer.

'The estate agent showed me the details of two more houses today,' Mother announced at tea. 'But one was far too expensive, and the other, when we went round to see it, wouldn't do at all. It would be all up and down stairs, as it is on four floors and very narrow. It looked as if it hadn't been re-

47

decorated since before the war.' And that was typical of house after house which she went to see. They all turned out to be unsuitable. We felt as if we were walking down a dead-end street with no possible openings.

Then the possibility of a house in Streatham arose. Mother came back from viewing it looking quite excited. 'It's not *too* remotely beyond our means, and it's *just* the right size. And we would be able to divide off part for our home with a separate front entrance.'

Negotiations appeared to be going smoothly and after a few weeks we felt the house was almost ours. Then one day when Mother was in Sevenoaks looking over a well-run old people's home, gathering all the advice she could, the phone rang. It was the estate agent. We had got him to put the call through to where Mother was. The matron kindly left her alone in the little office to hear what the agent had to say. 'I'm sorry, Mrs. Hoyte, but the Council have put an order of compulsory purchase on the house in Streatham. They want it themselves for an old people's home. There is nothing further we can do about it.' She put down the receiver, buried her head in her hands and burst into tears.

Had God deserted us now — this God in whom we professed to believe as a family? Did Christianity work sometimes, but at other times let you down?

A few rays of hope did glimmer for a moment through the dark clouds . . . The telephone rang again one day. It was the friend who was paying for Mary's radiography training. 'Would you like the use of our three-bedroomed house?' he asked. 'Father has to go to America on business for six months and he wants us to look after the family home in Henley. I know three bedrooms isn't very big for you all, but we won't need to take any of the things – there'll be blankets and linen and crockery — everything you need. And Richmond Park is just across the road.'

Mother jumped at the offer. Of course, it made our ultimate future no clearer, but it would tide us over for the moment. And when she worked it out, a three-bedroomed house would do fine for us for a while, as so many of us were away from home. Mary was working and the boys were at college or doing National Service. I had one more year to do at school before my 'A' levels, so a home was found for me in Chislehurst and I would go over to them for the weekends.

We were beginning to see that God *did* have it all worked out. The frustrating thing was that we could not see further than the next step. This still did not provide my parents with a job; and after six months, what then? Mother's words came back to me, 'That's the thing about the Christian life; you've got to take it on trust.'

So we must just trust God and carry on as if all were well? Easier said than done! Yet looking back, my parents have often said it was as though God was giving them a six months' holiday — a break from all the responsibilities of running a large hostel, a lull before they were immersed in the hard work and multiplicity of details involved in setting up an old people's home. If only they could have seen into the future, they might have relaxed more during those days.

'I can't imagine how we shall fit everyone in for Christmas,' Mother said to me when I came home one weekend. They had been in our new little home for over a month now. At first it felt rather like a doll's house. It was such a contrast to the huge silver-walled drawing-room we had been used to, with its wide view over spacious lawns, or the long dining-table which seated twenty-four people comfortably, overlooked by a fine row of dark oil paintings. 'You two girls can fit into the guest-room,' she went on. 'But even with mattresses downstairs we haven't room for the four boys to stretch out. Stephanie and Beth want to come, and Marlies. We can't possibly manage eleven people.'

Stephanie and Beth were two friends about my age who were at boarding-school in Sevenoaks. Stephanie's father was a government doctor in Kenya and Beth's parents were missionaries working in Brazil. Mother acted as guardian to both of them. Marlies was a dear German girl who had helped us faithfully at Chislehurst. She had become almost one of the family and when she saw the strain my parents were under she promised that as soon as they found a house she would come and help us get started. All three were expecting to come 'home for Christmas' just as much as we were. How could we sleep so many?

On going home again a few weeks later I was met by Mary excitedly at the door.

'Guess what's happened! Mother had a letter from someone in Blackheath. We hardly really know them — they only met on the train going to Michael and Mary's wedding. But they have written to say that every time they pray, God keeps reminding them of us. They don't know why. They are going away for Christmas and wondered if we could make use of their house for a week. It's the very week which John gets off from the army, and when the others want to be home too,' she finished up triumphantly.

Sure enough the dates were perfect, exactly to the day which we needed. And who can describe our excitement at walking into the house to find eleven beds made up in the various bedrooms, a turkey in the 'fridge', a Christmas cake and many other stores in the larder with a large notice, 'Make sure you eat it all up!' and a beautifully decorated Christmas tree bedecked with presents for each one of us! They had even remembered a bone for our golden labrador.

Gleams of sunshine were breaking through the dark clouds. It was as if God were saying, 'You see how well I can take care of the details. Won't you trust Me for the overall pattern too? I have your future all worked out.'

Faith, in the Bible sense, is not just a passive sitting back and letting God do it all. It involves our active co-operation. But it does take the anxiety out of a time of uncertainty. It removes the sense of strain when we do not know what the future holds.

The six months near Richmond Park had almost expired before my parents found the right house. They had thought of all sorts of other ways of earning a living. In desperation Father even went down to the local paint factory to see if they would take him on as an ordinary labourer. But he was over sixty-five, and not wanted. They kept coming back to the conviction that they should start an old people's home.

One cold February Saturday, those of us who were home for the weekend took the Green Line bus out to Reigate. My parents wanted to show us the house which they believed might be the right one. Situated in the shelter of the North Downs, this little town is surrounded by miles of lovely Surrey countryside. We got off the bus at the High Street and walked for half an hour down one of the busy roads leading out of the town, and then over a lovely golf course studded with Scots pines. Bungee, our golden labrador, delighted at being let free after the long bus journey, bounded away through the trees and over the stubbly heather which bordered the closely cropped freeway.

A mile and a half out of town we walked through big dark wood gates and up the well-kept drive of the house which God had chosen to be our home. A beautiful Himalayan cedar towered on the front lawn, flanked by blue spruce and a bank of rhododendrons. On the other side, the house faced south, with terraced lawns dropping down to a sweeping meadow. Distant Box Hill could be glimpsed to the west. The wintry rays of the sun gleamed through all the main windows, so that even though the house was completely empty the chill was gone.

Just before 1900, Dungate Manor had been built by a former Lord Mayor of London for his invalid wife. Made by the best workmanship at the time, and with lovely level parquet floors over which an invalid chair could easily be pushed, it was ideal for an old people's home. We paused in the spacious oak-panelled entrance hall to decipher the crest over the great stone fireplace. 'Domine Dirige Nos' — the motto of the City of London — 'Lord Direct Us' — so suitable for us as a family. And this was where He had brought us!

We spent an excited half hour exploring everything. 'Look at the lovely drawing-room, with this long window seat — and see those dear little windows next to the fireplace through which you can glimpse the chalk downs.'

'Come and see. These french windows open on to a lovely terrace. Why, it's so sheltered you could almost sit out there now in the sunshine. Won't the oldies enjoy their garden chairs here!'

'Come on up the stairs! They're beautiful. Feel this lovely

51

wood that they're made of; and see, they've even got built-in seats halfway up in case the oldies get tired!'

Right the way up to the top we all went. The first floor had many good-sized bedrooms, and we could already picture one or two elderly people happily settled in each one. Then, behind a servants' door, was another flight of narrower steps leading to a second floor of smaller rooms which we could imagine would be for our own family use. After the explorations, we all sat on the long window-seat in the empty drawing-room and had a picnic lunch.

'But how about the price, Mother?' John, my youngest brother, asked. 'Surely this is far too good for us.'

'It was so wonderful, the day I came on my own,' she said. 'I went all round the house praying and praying. Was this to be the right place at last? And as I walked down the garden I saw a frail old lady. She was looking so worried and said, "Do you want to buy our home? They want to turn it into flats. I can't bear it to be turned into flats. I don't know what to do." So there and then I told her all about ourselves; how you had all come out of China with literally nothing, and how Father is too old to work. And all about our plan for an old people's home where elderly folk can be cared for and not just herded together ... I must have said lots more, I was so full of it all. Afterwards, she went and phoned our estate agent to ask just how much we could afford. I do not know what she was asking for originally, because it had been already taken off the market as sold and all the particulars were destroyed. But she said we could have it for £6,200.'

'We've got the £6,000 already,' burst in Mary.

'Yes,' Mother smiled happily, 'and Father's dear secretary, Brock, who hasn't *any* money to spare, is giving us the £200.'

Spontaneous praise and prayer ended our picnic lunch.

Chapter Five

Trials

'GO AND FETCH the hanger from the wardrobe now, dear, and then come and unzip me. I can never manage this dress on my own.' I did as I was told and waited, standing first on one foot and then the other. The brush and comb had to be produced and then put away in the right spot on the dressing-table. Then the manicure set had to be found. Slowly each ring came off the swollen old fingers and was placed in the correct box. The string of pearls was unfastened and put away. How I hated it all! This half-hour each morning and evening seemed to grow longer and longer. But the crippled old lady seated on the chair in front of me was our first guest. We were all running round in circles to make her happy! Later we learnt more wisdom and realised we had not the time nor the strength to hover round each 'oldie' interminably. Besides, it was much better for them to do as much as they could for themselves. But these were early days, and we were still fearful that no old people would want to come. Promising to be back at nine with a hot drink, I was eventually able to slip thankfully out of the room, and join the others downstairs.

Much had happened in the last few months. The friends who lent us the house near Richmond Park refused to allow us to pay anything for rent, lighting and heating. Their generosity overwhelmed us. On the other hand, for six months Father and Mother had not earned a single penny and their resources were almost down to rock-bottom. They had nothing with which to pay the solicitor's fees or the stamp duty on the house. Although in later years we were always full to capacity, in those early days it was difficult to find elderly people to come. All the money from the few guests was spent as soon as it came in;

when the books were balanced at the end of the first year we were down £300.

Yet gradually things worked out. Much to their delight, the guests were allowed to furnish their own rooms. They hated to part with well-loved furniture, and of course it helped us tremendously. Friends rallied round and lent us furniture. Some was only a temporary loan, but at least it was something until we could afford to buy new things.

When we first moved in we were completely without electricity. The house had been on an old D.C. supply. The Electricity Board saw the change of ownership as an opportunity to insist that we changed over to the normal A.C. But without an extra penny to spare, my parents were horrified at the sum they demanded. Fortunately the months of negotiating were the longer summer ones of May, June and July when lighting was very little problem. We just all went to bed when it became too dark. Four months passed before word finally came through that the Board would pay for the alterations and charge us only a fraction of the original figure. We were jubilant at this further answer to prayer.

I postponed going to college for a year so as to help all I could. Together with Marlies, we scrubbed and cleaned room after room, cooked, washed and ironed and carried trays. Gradually our new pattern of life took shape. The Home became known and more guests came. A full-time nurse joined the staff and a cook was found. So I was free to go to college the following October.

University days were wonderfully happy ones. I was at a small, residential college in London, five minutes' walk from Kensington Gardens in one direction and Holland Park in the other. Unlike most other London students, nearly all of us lived in, so we got to know one another very well. We played tennis in the summer, and held coffee parties round our cosy gas-fires in the winter. It was fun being in London where there was so much going on — theatres, cinemas, art galleries, shops. There never seemed to be enough time to get round to all we wanted to do.

I found the studies fascinating. Household science, which I

was studying, is a happy combination of practical subjects like cooking, with some more scientific ones like nutrition and physiology. Pure science, as such, appeared too abstract to me, but these were all subjects which caught my imagination and which I could see applied in everyday life. It was just the same as it had been at school, only more so. I found a whole world of knowledge opening up to me: the wonderful balance of the different mechanisms inside the human body, the microscopic marvels of the realm of bacteriology, the variety and complexity within the study of nutrition. By the time I was in my third year I could willingly have made a career of household science. But hadn't I felt as a teenager that God wanted me to become a missionary? This thought was often at the back of my mind. It was hard to be sure about it, hard to know if that incident so long ago was merely the result of a rather emotional conversation.

I remembered another evening too, while we had still been at Chislehurst. I was cycling home just behind Mary after our weekly Young People's Bible Study. Her thick golden plaits hung down almost to the waist of her dark coat, jerked with each swing of the pedals. I couldn't get some words out of my mind. As I watched Mary's legs steadily pumping round they seemed to keep time with them: 'You are not your own. You are bought with a price' — Not your own, bought with a price: my own legs kept time too as we sped home through the dusky evening. 'Not your own, bought with a price': that was what the Vicar had been speaking about. And it was true. Years ago I had given myself over to God. Diffident, unsure of myself and basically selfish — it was not much to offer Him, and certainly amazing that He should ever want me. But I believed Him to be real. As a family we had proved Him so often and found Him to be true. Moreover I was committed. Could I pull back now?

There was another persistently niggling thought which I could not avoid. The trouble was, I knew too much about missionaries! My parents had a host of missionary friends and kept in touch with many people in all parts of the world. And from my youthful viewpoint, to become a missionary was almost synonymous with giving up all hope of marriage. There seemed to be crowds of single lady missionaries, while single men were as rare as pearls in an oyster. I could picture them all again: rather severe-looking middle-aged spinsters, hair scraped into a tight bun at the nape of the neck, and long full skirts billowing with their energetic stride. I shuddered at the thought that I should ever become like that! Yet was I not heading that way? When I mentioned to any of the Christian fellows I was growing friendly with, that I was thinking about becoming a missionary, our relationship would grow noticeably chilly.

It was doubly annoying because we girls in the Christian Union had just been gloating over the fact that during our three years up at college we had got to know far more boys than the non-Christian girls! In spite of not attending the Saturday night 'hops' and other dances and socials which in those days Christians usually avoided, the Christian activities of Bible studies and weekend conferences had brought us far more lasting and worthwhile friendships with members of the opposite sex. I loved male companionship. I seemed to thrive on it. If there was one thing I could not bear, it was the thought of remaining a spinster all my days.

During my last long summer vacation I helped cook at a boys' camp and was much attracted to one of the officers. He appeared to enjoy my company too; until — well, I just knew I had to tell him. I knew it would not be fair to our whole relationship, and the sooner it was said, the better. So out it came: I felt God was calling me to become a missionary. Had he ever thought of it too? That dished it! His attitude noticeably cooled, and our budding relationship crumbled.

In my final year at college a decision had to be made. Between the hectic swatting for examinations, all my friends were applying for jobs. One was accepted by the World Health Organisation, another was going on to do food research. Maureen was due to get married and Jean planned to study for a Ph.D. What should I do?

I went away in March of that year to a small Christian Union conference I had helped to organise. Coming home, I found myself in the train next to the visiting speaker. Others of our party found seats further down, and the noise of the clanking wheels prevented our conversation being overheard. There are some people with whom one feels one can open up and share one's deepest feelings after a very short acquaintance. Our speaker was one of these. I found myself telling him about my uncertainties as to my missionary call and how I really could not face it anyway, because I hated to remain single.

He looked at me straight with his candid grey-blue eyes and asked, 'Elizabeth, if you believe in God, can't you believe that He loves you? Can't you trust Him to choose the very best for you? Don't you realise that He has made you? He knows you through and through. He knows what you need and what you don't need. If He has made you for marriage He will see that you get a husband; and if He has planned for you to remain single, He has a plentiful supply of all the extra grace that you will need. Can't you trust Him with your life, and leave it all to Him?'

Yes, that's what it all boils down to, I realised, as I continued the journey back alone. Was God trustworthy? Could I rely utterly on Him? As I looked back over my life — childhood in China, early days in England, my step-mother, our various homes and now college — I knew that God had never let me down. I knew I must take a deep breath and trust Him with this greatest longing I had ever known.

Everything did not fall into place at once, but I began to pray more definitely. 'If you want me to be a missionary, O God, please show me how best to train. And if you don't, please put something in the way.' It came to me that most missionary work is teaching. I needed to develop the ability to communicate, to express my thoughts clearly and simply. The best preparation for this would be to get a job as a teacher and to learn by actually doing it. I was still very nervous of standing up in public and hardly ever dared open my mouth in student-union meetings, though I had learnt to control my nerves in front of a sympathetic group such as the Christian Union. A year's teaching would surely help me to overcome this hurdle. And how thankful I was later, when addressing audiences of several hundred people in a foreign language, that this fear had been largely overcome.

In those days one could go straight into teaching with an honours degree without troubling to study for the Diploma of Education. My friends helped me scan the newspapers for teaching appointments and I sent off several applications. It is always disappointing to be turned down, and I found the initial refusals rather hard to bear, but a few weeks later I saw that God had been overruling events again. I had been applying to *schools*. Now a vacancy appeared on the staff of a new technical college in Reading. They needed someone with just my training, and it would give me much wider experience, working with a mixed staff and dealing with students from many different walks of life. During the interview for this job I felt clearly that God was right there in the room, helping me answer the questions. Everything that came up I was given the answer to, in a way which quite surprised me. I had seldom been so aware of God's direct help. And the answer came a few days later: I was offered the job. God seemed to be saying, 'You are heading in the right direction. I have it all worked out for you. This is just the sort of training you need before becoming a missionary.'

One of the teachers from my old school in Chefoo lived in Reading. I wrote to ask her help in finding digs.

'I've found just the place for you, Elizabeth,' she wrote straight back, and on my next visit to Reading she took me round to see Mrs. Gilkes, who was an elderly Christian lady, too frail now to go out much, but one who spent a good deal of her time in prayer. In the years to come she became one of my most faithful prayer supporters. I had no idea of all this when I first met her, only of her warm welcome, and of the pleasant attic room which she showed me, with low rafters and a wide view from the dormer window. Here I would be completely private on the top floor by myself; yet I would have the use of her bathroom and kitchen, and would be welcome in the lounge whenever I cared to put in an appearance. The house was within easy cycling distance from the technical college — ten minutes downhill there and fifteen minutes back — as well as being near her church, where I soon became a member. Later they also promised their support and sent me out as one of their own missionaries, even though I had spent only nine months with them.

A job, a home-from-home, and a supporting church: the threads of the pattern were beginning to take shape. I was beginning to find out for myself the thrill of trusting God and seeing Him work things out for *me* personally.

That summer we had a family holiday in Connemara on the west coast of Eire. Friends lent us their isolated cottage, five miles along the sea road out from Clifton. Memories come back of exploring the lonely coastline; bathing from a secluded cove with no one else in sight; scrambling up the Nine Bens with only the sheep for company; fishing for supper in the stream near the cottage, the dying sun tingeing the water a delicate pink. My sister Mary baked us all home-made brown bread, its recipe learnt from the old woman who lived in the one other cottage in sight of our front door. The recipe began: two saucers of wholemeal flour and one of white. It was the first time I had heard of that measurement, but the end result was most satisfying. The delicious smell of that crusty bread is still with me.

One day the postman stopped for a long chat, and, just before leaving, produced a small bundle of letters. They must have been accumulating in Clifton until someone had the energy or inclination to cycle the five miles out to us. One letter was for me, and what I read filled me with dismay. I was planning to travel straight from Connemara to organise the cooking at a large camp, and one of my helpers was writing to say she now found she could not come! How could I possibly find someone else at the last moment? Even if I did write to one of my friends, her answer would never reach me in time. And I knew we could not possibly manage with one cook short. It was the first time I had been in a tight spot, needing urgent, immediate action but with no possibility of being able to do anything about it. The only thing I could do was to pray. At the back of my mind was the thought that as soon as we arrived back in England I had better put in some long-distance phone calls. But to whom? Thinking quickly around the various possibilities, I realised that each college friend had already organised a busy summer programme. None would be likely to be free.

What happened took me completely by surprise. Not seeing *how* God could answer my prayer, I had little faith that He would; so the answer came unexpectedly. Bathing next day from our favourite secluded beach, we were almost indignant when we saw another car parked on the headland and a small holiday party make their way across *our* golden sand. We had almost come to think of this cove as 'private property'! I was stooping to collect our disorderly possessions, so as to pile them near together — 'you never know what strangers may be like' — when a shout from John made me look up.

'Why David, fancy seeing you here! Well, this is great!' David turned out to be one of John's undergraduate friends from Cambridge, who happened to be holidaying in this area with his family. And Mary, his sister, whom we had never met before turned out to be God's answer to my prayer!

After a delightful day's picnicing together I found out that she was doing nothing the following week and would be delighted to come and help cook. 'If you dare take me on,' she added, 'I've never done anything like that before!' I was in no position to turn up my nose at anyone. Besides, I enjoyed her company enormously. So we made arrangements where and when to meet.

As both families parted that evening, John said to me, 'David has been praying for his sister for a long time. I wonder if God hasn't especially allowed this to happen.' And when Mary became a Christian towards the end of the week of camp, we all marvelled at God's perfect planning. It gives a special thrill to be a spectator when such things are happening.

I would not advise anyone to teach for only one year. All your lecture material must be prepared from scratch — and then never used again. It was a hectic time. I was constantly rushing to meet deadlines and learning how to make use of filmstrips and tape recordings when I had not had time to prepare the lesson properly myself. I began to realise how academic my knowledge was and how little real practical experience I had. Often I felt my teaching was all a matter of bluff: keep one lesson ahead of the students, but pretend you know everything!

Yet I enjoyed it as well — at least most of the time. After all, the students at a technical college are there because they want to learn. There were no problems of discipline to trouble me, such as I might have faced in a school. Teaching two evening classes a week gave me late mornings on other days and a very flexible programme. All the demonstration-dishes which I cooked at college I could take home to eat, so housework in my digs was cut down to the minimum.

Fortunately I was not teaching any examination subjects, or I dread to think how the students would have fared! The other members of staff in our department were all so experienced, and I felt a complete novice beside them. The evening-class students were mostly my seniors by several years, but there was a happy spirit among both students and staff and we all enjoyed our work immensely.

I think I must have been the only member of staff who arrived on a bicycle. I sensed that the head of our department did not consider it quite proper: if you had no car, you should bus or walk! But I had planned just this one year to earn enough money to take me through two years at Bible College; so I was saving every penny I could.

The cycling was not the only way in which I appeared odd. My religious views were soon known, and one of the men on the staff delighted to bait me. I had fair hair and a high colour which flushed disastrously at the least provocation. It was most annoying.

'How can you believe that five little bread rolls were enough to feed five thousand people?' he taunted. 'Can't you see, the little boy shared what he had brought? Others did the same; and with everyone sharing it around, there was enough for all.'

I was floored. I had never heard that explanation. On the spur of the moment I forgot that the story specifically says 'they had nothing to eat' and the little boy's luncheon was apparently the only food the disciples could find in all that crowd!

But of course it does not matter whether or not other people had happened to bring some picnic as well. The key question was, 'Is Jesus Christ God?' If He is, it would not be difficult at all to feed five thousand people; but if He is not, the whole of the Christian faith collapses.

During those days I had the heartbreaking experience of turning down someone who had been asking me to marry him for a number of years. We had known one another very well since childhood. He had been out of the country, but had written frequently and shared deeply in his letters.

'How foolish I am being,' I kept telling myself, 'when I want marriage so badly. After all, he *is* a Christian, and he's not opposed to missionary things. He just doesn't feel he should join the society I am heading for. For once it's somebody asking *me*, instead of me hopefully looking round! And I am really very fond of him.'

It is a shattering experience to see a big strong man cry. All my instinct was to put my arms around him and shield him from the pain. What held me back? Somehow the conviction was deeply there, that he was not God's partner for me, fond as I was of him. We walked off in opposite directions. It was the only thing to do. And I found my relief in tears when I reached the shelter of my own little attic room.

I decided to apply to a missionary training college which was just for women. It was too distracting to be constantly thinking about marriage. It left me so churned up and feeling so lonely: much better to concentrate on training for the two years and learn all I could. There was still so much in me which made me dissatisfied. I longed to grow to know God better. If I was to be on my own in some remote place I would need to be sure I had a God whom I could trust.

Chapter Six

Bible College

IT WAS MY first morning at Bible College. We had all spent an hour in prayer and reading our Bibles and now the whole college was to be cleaned before we had breakfast. I had been allotted one of the staff bedrooms to do. Another member of staff showed me where it was.

'When you dust a room,' she began, 'you work systematically round, starting from the door. Remove all the loose articles from the desk here. Dust it thoroughly. Then dust each article and put it back in the right place.'

I felt my blood beginning to boil. What did she think I had been teaching for the past year? I wasn't a schoolgirl! I bit my tongue and said nothing.

Missionary training was to be a mixture of experiences. Perhaps it was because I had so much to learn in my own character that a number of things rubbed me up the wrong way. Yet these were offset by much that was good.

The Chairman of our Council lectured on church history and Christian doctrine. He opened up whole new worlds to me, tracing the thread of Bible-based Christianity right through the centuries. With my strong Protestant background I had the naïve picture of there being practically no Christians from Constantine's era to the time when Martin Luther wielded his hammer on the Wittenberg church door!

The lectures on Christian doctrine set my heart glowing. What a God we worship — so great, majestic and powerful; yet so tender in His love and care for man! Afterwards I would sit under the languid branches of the weeping willow by the river watching the snow-white swans glide gracefully by, and in my heart sing a paeon of praise to God who was becoming so real to me.

Sheer love of people and the ability to get along with them were the qualities which shone in our Vice-Principal. I was privileged to be in the team she led which ran a weekly women's meeting. It was obvious she cared about each one who came. She greeted them with questions which showed her intimate knowledge of their family and home circumstances. And as she spoke in the meeting she had the ability to draw them all together through the mutual bonds of womanhood. They sensed she knew their days of tiredness, their family heartaches and problems about the future; and as one who was experiencing these very same things she pointed them to her own source of strength: 'God knows and loves and cares. Open your hearts to Him and see the difference He will make.'

Her love for others impressed me all the more because I was not particularly interested in people. Study, yes! And even giving up my future to become a missionary, yes! But people as such, no — especially uninteresting old folks, living in dingy, stuffy flats and out of touch with the modern world. I had not yet discovered the richness to be found in human relationships. Perhaps it was because I was still so unsure of myself and had seldom found real satisfaction in communicating with other people. At school, apart from two or three friends, my chief delight had been study. College had been the same. Books were so much more predictable than people. They never had their 'off days' and one could not hurt them unintentionally. It was the accidental hurting of others which was largely the trouble. I was frequently so tactless, saying something quite innocently, only to find the other person had taken offence. Again and again it happened, until I found the best thing to do was to thicken the shell around me and not to share deeply with anyone. Underneath there was the longing that others should approve of me. My perfectionist ideals were forcing themselves to the front again. I wanted to be the best at everything, to be highly thought of, to be one to whom others would look up. Yet I found that I might shine in the lecture-room, but certainly not elsewhere! My big desire to make a good impression just showed itself in selfishness. If we are always wondering what others are thinking of us it is bound to show. The trouble was, no amount of studied good behaviour could alter the basic *me*. In fact the more I tried, the more artificial it became, and the bigger the jolt when I realised I had done something tactless again.

'Oh, Gwen, what's the matter?' I said one evening. 'Haven't you been with your fiancé all day?' It was nine-thirty p.m. on a Saturday and we all had to be back in College. Gwen had just arrived with her eyes filled with tears. I so longed to get married that I could see no further than the joy it must be to her to get engaged.

'O, you'll *never* understand,' she burst out. 'I want him; and we've waited so long; and the Mission says we can't get married for another year.' She rushed out of the room and up-stairs.

'There, I've done it again!' I thought miserably. 'Jealous of her because she has a fiancé, but not understanding at all how she is feeling!'

Cynthia was my closest friend at Bible College. She told me one day she was praying for what the Bible calls an under-standing heart, a heart that really loves others and is sensitive to them. She had realised the importance of caring for people; but I was stuck at the earlier stage of wanting others to approve of *me*. Still engrossed with the impression I was making on them, I could not see that the answer was to forget myself and start to love.

I went back one term feeling utterly miserable. The holiday had not been all it should have been and now coming back to college only meant I was face to face with myself again.

'Nice to see you back, Elizabeth,' one of the staff greeted me at the door. 'How are things?'

'O, pretty miserable,' I said half-heartedly, 'but never mind.'

Seeing the look on my face she hesitated.

'Wait a moment. I think I've got something for you.'

She came downstairs a moment later with a small piece of paper in her hand. It was from a tear-off calendar which gave a verse from the Bible for every day. I looked down at the words chosen for this day and read, 'I will do better unto you than at the beginning. And ye shall know that I am the Lord.' God's pledge that, even if I was fed up with myself, He had not finished with me!

I smiled gratefully and went upstairs.

The Missionary Society I was applying to recommended that, before going overseas, their new workers should attend the Wycliffe Language Course. Here during seven intensive weeks of study the principles of language-learning were taught. I knew others who had greatly benefited by this short course and advertised it strongly amongst students who, like me, were finishing at Bible College that summer. Then, much to my consternation, I found that the course was due to begin a week *before* college ended.

I went to the Principal. 'Would we be allowed to leave early, or could something else be done about it?' I did not imagine that the college dates might possibly be shortened at the request of a mere student, and my agitation must have shown clearly. Much to my dismay, it was taken almost as a personal insult. Could I not trust the staff to have my best interests at heart? I was doubting their love and concern when I reacted in such a way. This had not been my intention at all. Startled, I realised that once again I had been thought to be tactless and had caused unnecessary offence. I felt more depressed than ever. I seemed quite unable to predict how people would respond to things I did or said. What *was* the use of trying? The Christian life just did not seem to work. God might be real enough to help in practical, material ways, but when it came to things that mattered — personality, character, temperament — He appeared powerless to make any difference.

I left Bible College under a cloud, feeling a complete failure. I did not want to look at the ordinary certificate I had been presented with on the last day of term. I wanted the honour one. I wanted to be the best, and I obviously had not been. There was so much I had wanted to do; but it never worked out. I only went on with the next step towards being a missionary because I knew I *had* to, not because I had any inclination to, and certainly not because being a missionary was in any way 'higher' than any other calling from God. How He could eve use anyone as useless as me I could not imagine; but He had called me and I had to go on.

My one year's teaching had enabled me to save more than enough money to cover the first year's missionary training. The college only asked the students to pay half the amount required, and together as a big family we prayed for the rest of the money. Term by term it had been a miracle to watch it coming in. Then for myself, I found I had enough for my second year's fees — not through anything spectacular, but just because my parents were able to repay the loan on our old people's home. We six children had all been left money by our grandfather, which came through just when capital had been needed to purchase Dungate Manor. Gradually Father and Mother were able to repay each one of my older brothers and sisters and my turn 'happened' to come during my second year at Bible College. It was sufficient also to cover the cost of the Wycliffe Language Course; so I thankfully went on to that, believing it to be the next step for me.

Little actions of love can do so much to heal a sense of inadequacy. For instance, when we arrived at the Candidates' Course for the Overseas Missionary Fellowship, each of us found a fresh green plant to welcome us in our rooms. They had been grown by a retired worker, who suffered badly with an enormously swollen leg owing to elephantiasis contracted overseas. The little touch of green would lift my spirits every time I looked at it. I loved all garden things, and the outlook from the window across the grey chimney stacks of London's East End was particularly depressing. What a difference those fresh green leaves made to me!

The Women's Candidates Secretary was another person who knew just how to say the right word. I sensed that she believed in me and cared. It made all the difference.

Another highlight from those months before sailing came after our farewell meeting in Glasgow. Our Scottish Secretary said to the two or three of us who spent that night in Glasgow, 'I'll meet you tomorrow and show you some of the sights.' Sure enough he did. We had a day of breath-taking beauty, sweeping along the shores of Loch Lomond as far as Loch Katrine, with a far-off glimpse of the Trossachs in the distance. He was a busy man and this could have been his free day, but he spent it giving us an unforgettable experience.

As we were driving back to Glasgow that evening he said, 'I think there's still ten minutes to go before the Art Gallery closes. Would you like to see Salvador Dali's painting of 'Christ on the Cross'? I had of course seen reproductions of the masterpiece, but was not prepared for the effect the more-than-life sized painting would make: the Son of God gazing out over His world, from His cross. It was so vivid I could have stretched forward and gently touched Him on the back of His shoulder — but the agony and yet strength in that body held my hand back. I gazed at the painting, awestruck. It was as if that magnificent tragedy was happening once again before my own eyes. How greatly Jesus must have loved me! How staggering that He had done it for *me*!

April 1960 came, and with it, that for which I had been preparing for so long. I was with a large party of new missionaries sailing for Singapore.

Father, my oldest brother and my sister Mary motored down to Southampton to say goodbye. Looking back, how can one analyse the emotions which strive for predominance at a time like that? The tingling excitement at setting out on a great new adventure; the haunting worry: would I ever see Father again? (He was seventy-five years old now.) The ache of parting with Mary — she had helped me so much as an older sister; the unexpected delight at finding our cabin full of flowers, and the crowds of friends who came to wish one well. The momentary thought, 'I'll be all on my own now. How shall I ever cope?' The elation at the glimpse into the luxury lounges and dining-room. Exhilaration, nagging doubts, anticipation, fears and homesickness — each surged like the waves of the sea across my emotions, momentarily gaining the mastery and then giving way to another.

Then the ship's hooter sounded. The visitors had to leave. The engines throbbed more strongly and slowly we drew away.

That evening as we passed the Needles, silhouetted strongly against a darkening sky, I remembered the last time I had seen them. I had been leaning over a ship's rails that time also; but then it had been fifteen years before, when England was still an unknown country to me. How much had happened in that time! *Then* I had only known God as a second-hand experience. I had watched Him at work as if from a distance. *Now* I knew for myself that He really existed, that He was someone I could be in touch with and who made a difference. But there was still a dissatisfaction: what about the things I saw inside me, which I longed to change but seemed powerless to remove? Could God deal with them too? And what about the future, when I might find myself all on my own, far from other Christian friends and support? Could God be utterly relied upon then? Was He really as great and as loving as He claimed to be?

Chapter Seven

Martin and Marriage

MARTIN TELLS ME we sat next to each other at supper on the first night of the Wycliffe Language Course. I have no memory of it; but that is perhaps not surprising, as it was 'love at first sight' for him, while it took me a whole year before I would say yes!

My first boy-friend had been broad-shouldered and fair-haired, a real Celtic giant. Martin was thin and dark and not at all used to girls — in fact quite awkward sometimes with us. Maybe I was not sufficiently sorted out in myself to respond at first, or maybe there were other things. Certainly marriage is one of the biggest decisions a person can ever make, far more binding than choosing a career or even joining a missionary society. So each time Martin asked me to marry him all my self-protective instincts came out, and I gasped and said, 'No.' And yet I wanted to get to know him better.

We had talked a little on the Wycliffe Course and even more on the O.M.F. Candidates Course. We saw one another occasionally in the remaining three months before we sailed, so that by the time we were on the ship we were getting to know each other fairly well. Three weeks on the luxury liner gave all the passengers plenty of leisure time. Our party enjoyed it to the full. Although we were travelling tourist class the food was excellent and there were plenty of facilities for recreation. We swam in the ship's pool, sunbathed nearby or played games during the day. At night we walked in the cool breeze, marvelling at the beauty of the far-off electric lightning or the star-studded sky overhead.

When we reached Aden we all took taxis up the rocky road which climbs to the rim of a gigantic extinct volcano and then falls sharply down into Crater City. Martin and I together explored the fascinating Queen of Sheba's water tanks. Tradition has it that the great Queen herself supervised the excavation of these huge terraced reservoirs to act as a water-supply for her city. They are imbedded in the walls of the far rim of the crater, and the view from the topmost tank across Crater City and out beyond to the harbour and sea was spectacular.

Hurrying taxis brought us quickly back to the jetty to catch the last ferry across to our liner. By then the sun was sinking in a magnificent blaze of oriental glory. We had never seen such a sunset before; it appeared as if the whole sea were ablaze and our ship caught in the centre of the holocaust. For a few brief moments we could do nothing but gaze and marvel. Then within minutes the glory began to fade, and the rapid subtropical twilight began to assert itself. The breeze from the water freshened and the spray from the prow of the little ferry tossed in our faces. We were glad to climb up the gangway before the rapid darkness swallowed the sea and harbour into night.

At Colombo, Martin and I explored the gem market. Rows of fascinating tent-like stalls lined the narrow streets, each one with a vendor begging us to step inside and examine his precious jewels dug up in the hills nearby. Fantasies of Arabian Nights jumbled with light-fingered pick-pockets in our imaginations. Weird Indian music shrilled through the dusk and little house-lizards appeared and chattered excitedly on the pillars of the Hindu temple. We were quite relieved to come through the other end without having lost a handbag or a wallet! Martin and I found our way down to the long sea wall and walked through the brightening moonlight, listening to the mysterious roar of the black waves as they pounded on the beach. Time to talk, and share, and grow to know one another . . .

At Bombay a missionary cousin of mine had arranged for an Indian friend to show our large party round the sights. Splashes of exotic colour from the great bougainvillea arches form my main memory of the city. For Martin it was being detained with the Indian friend at a police station! An official guide had accused our friend of illegally taking a party on a guided tour. Deadlock ensued while the officials waited for the expected white man's bribe. Martin refused to budge, and nearly missed the ship. The gangway was already pulled up before he finally made it. But his obstinacy had been rewarded, as his pocket was no lighter.

Penang brought our first taste of the Far East and for me the old beloved Chinese shouts and smells. How familiar it all appeared — the rows of Chinese characters above the shop doors, the little eating-stalls right on the pavement, the heavy loads carried on either end of a supple bamboo pole. Yet there was much that was different. The rickshaws were replaced by motorised trishaws. The large hoardings outside cinemas on every main street caught the eye. And what a mixture of races there was here — Chinese speaking a dozen different dialects, Malays, Indians and Westerners.

Martin and I took the funicular railway up the 2,000-foot peak to the top of Penang Hill. We visited the amazing Snake Temple and gazed at the pool of sacred tortoises, many of which were said to be over 100 years old. The massive golden Buddha in the innermost enclosure made our hearts ache for those who prayed to its lifeless form ... And between all this there was time to talk, to explore. Was marriage God's will for our lives?

Finally, Singapore, our destination! We were to spend four months here in orientation and language study; but first it must be decided to which country each new missionary would go. I had another of my attacks of cold feet and said 'no' again to Martin — this time finally, I thought. Although the Directors had wanted to send us both to Indonesia, they realised it would not be fair to ask us to study all day and every day together, just the two of us. So Martin was invited to prepare for Indonesia, while I would go to Taiwan and therefore would start the study of Mandarin Chinese.

In view of the fact that eventually I said 'yes' and had to start all over again on Indonesian, nearly a year behind Martin, one could ask, 'Does God make mistakes?' Here were two people praying about the biggest issue of their lives and sincerely wanting to know and follow God's will. Why did He not make it clear? Why were we allowed to walk along a 'wrong' path for so long? Surely this was a clear case of God letting us down.

Martin was perhaps harder hit than I was, although I felt baffled and unhappy enough. From the first day he met me he had prayed about our relationship, and felt repeatedly that God was making it clear that I was to be his bride. He had told the Lord that even though he loved me, if our marriage was not God's will for him he was ready to give it up. In all honesty he searched his motives. But the conviction only grew that I was the one. So how could I now give him a final 'no'? He felt his whole faith in God shaken to its foundations. He was staking his life on this God. He had travelled 7,000 miles in obedience to Him. He had given up a promising career as a Russian interpreter. His whole future was at stake. And now was God not to be trusted? Did He mock us when we most needed Him?

A man often has to fight his battles alone, while a girl can draw comfort from friends. Though I had always tried to run my own life and manage efficiently on my own, I now began to find how precious friendship can be. My shell began to crack: I could not preserve it any longer. The agony of knowing the pain I was causing drew me close to Cynthia and to the two girls I roomed with. How healing it was to let the tears come and not to try to hide anything! How good to feel the closeness of human love!

Through the darkness of these months Martin could find no solution to his dilemma. If God was mocking him, to whom then could he turn? He had already experienced the emptiness of life without God in the navy. He had seen through the hollow chit-chat of cocktail parties; he dreaded the empty materialism of a life geared to social success or the pursuit of wealth. He knew there was more in man than just these outward things, and he had only found satisfaction when he came in touch with God and entered into a deepening relationship with Him. All he could do now was to pray. 'O, God, I know You are real. I know You are there. I can't understand what

74

You are doing but I've just got to trust You. Somehow You have the whole situation in Your hands, although it looks such a mess to me.'

God was not making a mistake. We were both learning lessons we could not have grasped in any other way. Even my study of Mandarin was not wasted. Later in Sumatra it gave me entrance into the small Chinese Christian community in our town. I was able to use it in the selling of Chinese Christian magazines over the years. And the full cycle came when we eventually found ourselves in charge of the Singapore Language Centre and my small amount of Mandarin made all the difference to giving the new beginners a start on that difficult language.

But that is jumping ahead six or seven years. We could see none of this. We had to settle down to the sheer discipline of language study, and, although we lived at such close proximity, to try to avoid one another as much as possible.

Not long before the end of our four months at Language Centre everything changed for me. Of course, I felt Martin had changed too. He was quieter, more poised, more reliable — in fact I suddenly realised I could trust myself to him. That was it; you had to be able to jump off the deep end and know that the other one was there, to hold you and support you whatever might come, that you could trust yourself to him. Oh, the relief of letting go — the exhilaration of stepping into another's love and finding it there all around you, enfolding, and uplifting!

It was wonderful how everyone else entered into our happiness too. Cynthia's deep and unselfish joy amazed me — she seemed just as happy as if she were the one who was engaged. I knew I would not have been, but friendship was coming to mean more to me now. And our Director had tears of joy in his eyes when we went across to his office to tell him.

'Scrap your language study for the rest of the day and go to the Botanical Gardens instead,' he said. How well he understood our need to be alone for a few hours together to unwind! That evening at the central O.M.F. prayer meeting when the opening hymn was announced, all the Language Centre students smiled and exchanged glances. For me, it expressed exactly what I was feeling too, both towards Martin and towards our God who had not failed us:

> O love, that wilt not let me go,
> I rest my weary soul on Thee.

Now we were to understand in depth what Gwen had gone through at Bible College during her long engagement. O.M.F. had a rule, which has since been abolished, that all new missionaries should do two years overseas and reach a specified language requirement before being allowed to marry. There was much wisdom behind this decision, as the single worker is free to live in local homes and get close to the people, whereas a married woman may experience great difficulty in finding enough time for language study, and so become badly frustrated. However, there were also other difficulties which made the waiting time very hard; so, with some change in cultural outlook and with better language facilities now available, the rule has been abolished. Unfortunately, we were two of the unlucky ones who had to wait.

Martin's application for a visa to Indonesia had been sent off long before our engagement took place. As Indonesian visas were notoriously slow and could take anything from six to eighteen months to come through, plans had been made for him to continue language study at what was known as Malay House. This was a pleasant, modern house situated to the east of Singapore City on the edge of a large Malay *kampong* or village community, where those of our Mission who were attempting to reach the Malays could meet them and be able to make friends. As the two languages of Indonesian and Malay are so closely related, it was hoped that the senior missionary could give Martin some help with his study.

I, meanwhile, had been engrossed in the study of Mandarin. The visa wait seemed so long and I was enjoying Chinese so much that our Director thought I should continue for a further six months, living in a Chinese home in the city. At the end of that time I would take Martin's place at Malay House. If his visa had come through he would go straight to Indonesia, and if not he would have to move up to South Thailand, the only other country where missionaries were allowed to work amongst Malays. In Eastern eyes it was unthinkable that an engaged couple should both sleep under the same roof; it was therefore impossible for us both to be at Malay House at the same time.

So as the language course disbanded and our large circle of friends prepared to board train or ship for the far corners of East Asia, Martin and I were taken only a few miles across the city. I was shown into my room in the Chinese home and Martin driven on a further three miles to Malay House. It was a strange feeling, being able to communicate with the household only through a language I had learnt for a mere four months. Furthermore, while they were all out during the day I was left alone with the servant and I had no means of talking with her at all as she spoke a different dialect. It would have been easier if the family had spoken Mandarin naturally between themselves, but although they knew it fluently, it was the language of education and they preferred their own Hakka in the house. In fact, very few families speak Mandarin between themselves in Singapore. So I was left alone with my books and tape recorder to get on with it. After the hum of busy Language Centre, with classes taking place and friends to compare notes with, the contrast was complete! Relief came at the weekends when I was allowed to stay at our lovely Mission Home; if there was a spare room Martin could be there too. The increasing loneliness felt during the week made me long all the more for Friday nights.

Those were six months learning self-discipline. Each day I set myself goals in my study. At the end of the week I reviewed the progress made, and tried to set the standard even higher. It was the best way to keep myself consistently at it, and it meant that I was ready to take the second language examination by the end of the six months. Looking back now, I can see that no more effective way could have been found to show me that books and study were not everything. Friendship and human relationships were what I began to crave for. In the evening, when the lady of the house came home, she would give me my language lesson. I found she was someone with real spiritual needs and it was a privilege to talk and pray with her. On Sunday mornings I attended a Mandarin-speaking church and had the great joy of giving my testimony there before I left. Needless to say, it had first been corrected word for word by my teacher!

One Saturday morning Martin and I were asked to see the Director. 'As Martin's visa for Indonesia still shows no sign of coming through, I have made plans for him to go up to South Thailand,' he told us. 'I thought you would like a holiday first, as you may not be seeing each other for some time, so last night I phoned our bungalow in the Cameron Highlands. They are able to take you for two weeks. Martin will then continue north as far as Sungei Golok and you, Elizabeth, will come back to Malay House. The Secretary will make all the travel arrangements for you.'

We left his office in a whirl, excited at the thought of a holiday together but filled with dismay at the prospect of being so far apart. 'How long do letters to South Thailand take?' we asked the girl in our postal department. 'Oh, anything up to ten days,' she replied casually. 'It depends what part you're in. Some places are much more accessible than others.' We hurried off to look at a map. What sort of a place was the Cameron Highlands and what would it be like for a holiday? How would Martin get from there to Sungei Golok, and just where was that, anyway? And all the time I was thinking, 'Ten days for a letter to get there! Why, that's nearly three weeks before a reply comes back!'

Sungei Golok, we found, was a border town on the main railway which went up the east coast of Malaya. When Martin had settled in, he discovered that by taking a long walk back over the railway bridge, past Customs and Immigration, on to Malayan soil, he was able to post me a letter which arrived in only two days. He posted another later in the week at his local post office which usually took the ten days. It meant that his letters were arriving all out of order, but I did not mind. At least we were hearing from each other, and when the fast letter arrived Martin did not feel quite so far away.

Yet if I had been lonely in the Chinese home, I felt even more lonely now. 'Don't be ridiculous,' I used to tell myself. 'At least you're living with other missionaries now. You've got someone to talk to when you're bored with language study. You can have interesting conversations at mealtimes.'

But reasoning did not help. I felt as if part of me was missing all the time, that I was trying to manage without a vital limb. Weekends were worst. Martin and I had always gone out together and the time had flown by so quickly. But now, how should I spend my day off? I could not go down to the beach by myself — a white girl all on her own there would look very strange. The married couple I was living with naturally wanted some time alone to themselves and looked forward to their weekly outing together. 'If only they would take me with them, just *once*,' I would think.

Starting again on a new language was pretty depressing, even if it was the language which I really needed.

'I go to the market . . .

'You go to the market . . .

'She goes to the market . . .'

I had to work through it all over again.

Before we left for Singapore, our Women's Candidates Secretary had given us a vivid survey of her life in China. She described the tortuous Burmah Road over which she and her husband had finally escaped. It wound through jungles and over high mountains. Deep ravines had to be negotiated, and hairpin bends up high cliff-faces. Many accidents had taken place on the road, and at the worst spots a large sign showing a skull and cross-bones warned drivers to take great care. She said she wanted to raise some 'skull and cross-bones' for us as we set out on our missionary career. The first one she mentioned was self-pity.

This was the very point to which I had come: self-pity. How easy it was to pile up a list of everything which was difficult! How easy to allow oneself to be swamped by depressing thoughts, by always looking on the dark side of things! Outwardly I was making progress with the language, going visiting with my senior missionary, and getting to know our Malay friends. My English-speaking Bible class showed encouragement and I enjoyed meeting with a few of them who lived in our area for weekly Bible study and personal counselling. Yet inwardly I was deeply unhappy and filled with self-pity, and nothing I could do about it seemed to shake it off.

The one who told us about the 'skull-and-cross-bones' signs must have sensed how I was feeling, because she sent me a card: 'Learn how to go and receive God's rest more and more, until it's a constant habit. Bless you, perhaps I understand specially and love much.' And a note at the end of Daddy's letter helped also. 'God bless you, darling, and enable you to abide in Him — as in a house, with a roof above, walls around and floor beneath, and an atmosphere of its own.'

After we had been apart for six months, Martin's visa for Indonesia at last came through. We met for a glorious but brief holiday. Then he flew to Medan, the capital of Sumatra — further away than ever!

The Mission was running into difficulties over my visa application. The Karo Batak Church who were sponsoring Martin had written out their official invitation to me too; but the government reply came back, 'We have approved of one missionary going to that area; we cannot consider allowing another one so soon.' It was pointed out that this was Martin's fiancée applying, but the answer was, 'Engagement is not legally binding and therefore we cannot recognise it.' It appeared that we should have to be married before my visa application could even be started, but Martin and I had still not been overseas for the two years which our Mission required. The waiting seemed endless.

One hot afternoon, I was curled up on the couch by the open doorway of Malay House, trying to get what breeze I could. The heavy scent of the fragrant white frangipani tree drifted slowly through the house. The others were all studying, and only I reacted to the sound of the postman coming up our drive, and the smack of a bundle of letters landing on the tiled floor. I shot out of my room to see if there was one with an Indonesian stamp. 'Nothing,' I thought despondently, 'only a couple of local ones.' Hating to get back to study, I opened the local one, which was addressed to all of us: the Mission's Fortnightly Newsletter. This was better than nothing; and at least it was cooler sitting out there than in my room!

What I read made me gasp. It was a summary of the decisions of the recent Overseas Council. One of the items was to the effect that the two-year wait before marriage was now to be shortened to one year after leaving Language Centre, provided the necessary language requirements were passed. We had left Language Centre more than a year ago. That meant we could get married right away — tomorrow if we wanted! I could hardly believe my eyes.

'Nancy, Elsie, come and read this', I called, 'the marriage rule has been changed. We can get married!' They rushed out to read the news for themselves and to share my joy.

But it was easier said than done. It is not easy to arrange a wedding when one partner is in another country. We had originally thought of being married in Indonesia. Friends of ours had done this. Their sponsoring church gave them a wonderful wedding, Indonesian style, with feasting and a wayang show all laid on. It made them feel very much part of the church they were working with. But the Indonesian Government's refusal to accept my sponsorship had made us realise that Martin would have to come to me.

News from him in reply to my excited letter was not encouraging. No O.M.F. missionaries were leaving the country just now because of a tax-clearance problem. The Mission had been registered as a charity and as such had not paid tax. Recently some official had objected and said we were *not* a charity and ought to be paying tax. Our Director in Jakarta was doing his best to sort out the problem, but in the meantime, no one could obtain an exit/re-entry visa because, to do so, it was necessary to prove that one had paid all tax due up-to-date. Such problems were liable to take months before they were resolved, and in the meantime there was nothing we could do.

I reached the depths of depression. After all this waiting, when we should have been able to get married, we were completely stuck. The other engaged couples from our group made their wedding plans. It was hard to enter into their joy. At one point the Mission suggested we should get married by proxy, so that at least my visa application could be *started* on the grounds of the marriage certificate. I remembered glumly that it had been a whole year after Martin's application had been launched before *his* visa came through. Then even the proxy wedding was ruled out. It was found to be illegal for British subjects outside a British colony. It all looked so black that I would sit in my room and just cry. The other girls tried to help, but it was no use. The tears would come. I could not stop myself. I could not shake out of it. Praying or reading my Bible seemed not to make the slightest difference.

Then a letter came from Martin saying his Director suggested that he could try to obtain an exit re-entry visa in spite of the tax-clearance problem. 'Go to all the other offices first,' he was told, 'but when you are at the tax office, you must not pay a cent or it will be establishing a precedent, and we shall all have to pay after that.' Martin suggested that I fix a wedding date and go ahead with making plans, and that together we should trust God to help him get out of the country. It did not appear very promising and was not at all what I had pictured for a wedding. My parents were far away: I would have to make all the plans myself — invitations, hymn-sheets, flowers, reception: letters to Indonesia took so long it was impossible to consult on all the details. And having done all that, I had no certainty that the bridegroom could even be there!

The skull-and-cross-bones flag of self-pity waved strongly in the breeze.

But I was forgetting I was part of another family — God's family; there really were those who cared. The wife of one of the directors at headquarters was just the 'mother' I needed. She invited me to rest up in her attractive little guest-room — just sleep and unwind and talk and be loved. 'Now you enjoy it all,' she said; 'you'll never have another wedding, so let's get all the fun we can out of preparing for it! You can't do anything about the visa, so it's no good worrying. Let's settle down and sort through what has to be done!'

Under her loving and helpful touch everything began to fall

into place. We sent out the invitations and chose the hymns. We walked together across the Botanical Gardens to see a beautiful church, cool and fragrant from the scent of the dark wood pews — and booked to have the wedding there. We imagined it decorated and decided where pots of flowers would stand. We went in her car down-town and ordered the flowers: deep red gladioli heads mixed with scented gardenias for me, and mixed carnations for the bridesmaids.

So much turns on one's attitude. Fun is much more what one puts into life than what one gets out of it. In spite of the uncertainty about Martin's visa, as she helped me count my blessings instead of looking at all the difficulties, I found the enjoyment coming back.

My sister Mary flew out from England to be one of the bridesmaids. It is a separate story of God's miracles, how she was able to come and how I was helped to find her a job so that she could stay on in Singapore; and God provided a lovely home with Christian friends where she could live. This couple helped in every way possible: the husband took a set of beautiful coloured photos of the wedding and the wife helped with the decorating of the hall for the reception. Cynthia, my friend from Bible College, promised to come down from our Mission School in the Cameron Highlands where she was teaching. She was the other bridesmaid. We fixed the date as late as possible in her holiday — Wednesday January 31st.

On Saturday January 27th, Martin received the news we hardly dared hope for: his exit re-entry visa had been granted. He had been to the tax office several weeks before and the official there signed his papers without a murmur — no mention of the tax due! All the papers had then been hurriedly forwarded to Jakarta and now at last they were back. But it was Saturday. All offices were closed. He would have to wait until Monday morning before picking the visa up. He could not even book a seat in a plane until he could show the airways official that he was allowed to leave the country. What if all the seats were taken?

First thing on Monday, he was round to collect his visa, then over to Garuda Airlines to book his seat: there were flights on

Tuesdays, Thursdays and Saturdays — only one flight left which would enable him to make the wedding! And there was a seat still vacant! Joyfully he cabled me that he would be arriving the next day. With just twenty-four hours before the wedding was due to take place we were in each others' arms, knowing that once more God had not let us down. We were walking on air as we raced off to complete the civil wedding at the Registrar's Office and then up to the Mission Home to deal with the last-minute preparations.

How amazingly everything had fallen into place, and what perfect timing! There was only one small dark cloud: tomorrow's wedding certificate would be just the *start* of my visa application. If it were to take months, as everybody else's had, Martin would have to go back to Sumatra alone and we should once more be parted. But everything was too wonderful just then for us to take any notice of a little cloud like that. We were together again and here was our wedding day. We were up in the clouds!

The impossible *did* happen — how, we never knew: but twelve days later I had my visa for Indonesia stamped into my passport. It had never happened before or since. When together we stepped on to the tarmac of Medan airport and Martin handed my passport to the immigration official, he looked at the stamp, amazed.

'How did you manage to get a visa so quickly?' he asked. And when he saw our smile he added, 'It must have been a *mujizat* — a miracle!'

Chapter Eight

Indonesia

'WELCOME TO INDONESIA!' Sybil's friendly American drawl
greeted us at the door of her home. Her three children, all under
five, tumbled out to say hello to Uncle Martin. He had been
living with them for six months and they knew him well.
Plump and lively, their fairness contrasted strongly with the
dark face of the Indonesian woman who helped look after
them.

'*Selamat datang* — welcome,' came the warm greetings from
the amah and the cook, as we shook hands all round and I
attempted my first stumbling sentences of Indonesian to a real
Indonesian. It was not so very different from the Malay I had
been learning, but there were some important changes I must
make straight away, as I soon discovered. 'How many children
do you have?' I tried to ask the cook. She stared at me,
horrified, and Sybil laughed. 'You asked her how many slaves
she keeps! That word is "slaves" not "children", here.' But
there was plenty of opportunity to learn Indonesian, as we
heard it spoken all around us.

'We've sent out invitations for a welcome-gathering for you
this evening,' Sybil's husband told us. 'We thought people
might like to meet the new bride. Then tomorrow I'll help
Martin start your tour of the offices to get Elizabeth's papers
straight. If you can get through by the end of the week you
should be able to move up to your own home in Kabanjahe on
Monday.'

'Why should papers take a whole week?' I asked. The
efficient offices in Singapore had been my only experience.

They all laughed. 'You'll soon find out,' Sybil said. 'You go
to one office and the man you want to see hasn't come in that

day: it's his granny's funeral. Or, if he is in, he can't sign anything unless you have a Mr. X's signature first, and he's away working in the fields all day to make a bit of money to supplement his inadequate pay.'

'And it's not only that,' her husband broke in; 'the recent rebellion by Sembolong and his troops has only just been squashed. This is a military area. You will need to have papers from the army and the police, as well as the usual residence pass, before you are allowed to stay. Don't worry,' he added, seeing my look of helplessness, 'I know the ropes and Martin is becoming well acquainted with these offices too! We'll see you through them all.'

I thought gratefully what a difference it made to belong to a missionary society where there were others with more experience to give advice.

That evening we all prepared for the welcome-gathering. All the available chairs in the house were crowded into the living-room. The dining-table was hardly visible under the dishes of curried savouries and sliced juicy tropical fruits. The children appeared with faces rosy and shiny from scrubbing, and the adults showered and changed into their best clothes. But the minutes ticked by; then half an hour — an hour, and only one friend appeared. He lived next door and arrived smiling soon after the appointed time. He slipped off his sandals at the door and shyly sat down on the nearest chair, while Sybil's husband chatted to him to set him at ease. We all took it in turns to talk to him, but the conversation dragged noticeably. Where was everyone else? Why weren't they coming?

After two hours Sybil felt we had better make a beginning on the refreshments so that the children could go to bed. The iced drinks had grown tepid and the fragrant dishes seemed to have lost their flavour from lying around so long. Or was it that we were all niggled with the unspoken question: 'Why hadn't people come?'

It was only two or three weeks later that Sybil began to receive apologies from friend after friend whom she had invited. Then it gradually dawned on her what had happened. She had posted the letters instead of delivering them by hand personally. Although the addresses were all within a five-mile radius it took weeks for the letters to arrive! So only the friend next door had known about the gathering in time.

Ginting, as we came to call him, dropped in a few days later to welcome me. Short, stocky, self-assured and in his early thirties, he was the General Secretary of the Karo Batak Church which had invited our help. He was one of only seven ministers for this large group of 20,000 Christians, scattered in over one hundred congregations throughout the Karo area of North Sumatra. The church had been started by Dutch missionaries before the turn of the century and had shown very slow growth in its early days. The Karos were suspicious of ulterior motives, as they knew the Dutch Government had been behind the missionaries' arrival. The Colonial Government wished to develop the rich volcanic soil as a huge market-garden concern. They therefore sent in the missionaries to establish schools and churches, hoping that in this way the indigenous people would be more amenable to their development plans.

During the war for independence from Holland (straight after World War II) nearly all Dutch personnel had been thrown out of the country. The Karo churches began to grow after an initial period of great difficulty, with no funds to pay their full-time workers and suffering under the stigma of having been friendly with the Dutch. Independence eventually brought new strength. They realised they were desperately short of man-power, yet were reluctant to call in missionaries again in case they should once more assume control of the church. Very tentatively their leaders approached our missionary society, the Overseas Missionary Fellowship, requesting help, with the proviso that the missionary appointed would have no power over their administration or finance. It was just at that time that we arrived in Singapore, and Martin was chosen to be the one to go. The Karo Church would provide him with a furnished house in Kabanjahe, their main town, and the Mission would be responsible for his financial needs.

Things move slowly in the East and now nearly two years later we were at last ready to meet their request. Ginting told us we were to be officially welcomed at the Karo church in Medan that Sunday morning, and the following day we should take the bus up to Kabanjahe. They were expecting us in our new home by twelve noon.

Early next morning Ginting appeared again unexpectedly. He hurriedly consulted our senior missionary. I missed practically all that was said but sensed something serious had happened. Martin and I found ourselves bundled into the back of the church jeep and then we were hurtling through the streets of Medan to pick up first one church official and then another. Neither of us liked to admit to Ginting that we had not understood what was the matter, and as the conversation in the jeep was all in Karo, not Indonesian, we could not follow any of it.

'I think someone must have died,' Martin whispered to me, 'but I'm not sure who.'

The jeep swung out of the city and along the straight, dusty road which led towards the distant mountains.

'That's where Kabanjahe is,' Martin said. I peered between the heads of the men in front of me to get a better view. 'See where the skyline seems to dip in a sharp "V"? The mountain road goes through there and on to the top of the plateau.'

I gazed at the blue haze which formed the predominating outline of the long line of hills and picked out the point he indicated. But we were not to go as far as that. Three-quarters of an hour later, Ginting stopped the jeep in a small town called Pancur Batu. We all climbed out stiffly and were shown into the front room of a house which stood by the roadside. The windows were so small, and there were so many people crowded inside, that it took our eyes a moment to adjust after the glare of the bright sunlight outside. Yes, it must be a funeral. Rush mats had been spread out on the floor to seat nearly fifty people, who crowded together cross-legged, men on one side, women and children the other. Those nearest the door did their best to edge up a little so that the Revd. Ginting and the men folk could sit down. I was directed over to the women's side and picked my way as best I could over to a tiny space

88

which was indicated. After the fresh breeze in the jeep the heat inside felt unbearable.

Gradually my eyes made out a small group at the other end of the room. They were softly moaning and swaying backwards and forwards. It was the women of the family, gathered round — could it really be? Yes, it was — the corpse laid out full-length on the matting. The body was covered with the traditional Karo hand-woven cloth but the face had been left clearly visible for all to see. Every now and then one of the women leant forward to brush the flies off. I shuddered. Who was he? Where were we? Who were all these poeple I was now with?

Martin had been talking in low tones with Ginting. He now made his way over to our side of the room. Etiquette or not, he must have a word with me. Excusing himself, he squatted down amongst the women and said quietly, 'It's the Revd. Barus who has died. Now they have only six ministers left in the whole church. He woke feeling fine yesterday morning and was taken ill about mid-day. By evening he was dead. They think it's cholera. There've been some other cases.' And then, seeing that some tea was being poured out, he added, 'Mind you don't drink any of that,' and picked his way back to join the men. The tea had been made straight in the kettle, the largest receptacle the family appeared to own. Three or four chipped enamel mugs were being passed around and the guests would drink, passing the empty ones back for re-fills with no thought of washing them. Knowing that cholera was carried by drinking water, I made a pretence at having a sip when the mug came my way, but did not allow it to touch my lips. We were all thirsty after our long drive and the heat seemed to grow greater as time passed, but to drink anything would have been folly.

After a time someone stood up to speak. It was all in Karo, so it was useless my attempting to understand it. He harangued the crowd for ten to fifteen minutes while everyone listened stoically. Then another man spoke, and another. Some of the children were going in and out. Nobody was really listening. One young mother unbuttoned her blouse and fed her little baby. The pretty dark face, bent lovingly over the tiny form, made a beautiful picture. The old women were passing round plaited bags of betel nut. I watched, fascinated. They took out a shiny green leaf, gently smoothed it between their fingers, and then placed in the centre a tiny shaving of betel nut and a pinch of some white paste. Some added a little dried tobacco. Deftly the concoction was rolled up between the fingers and popped into the mouth. They settled back happily to chew, their saliva gradually turning a rich red through the juices which were expressed. It obviously gave them a great deal of satisfaction. I studied their old, gnarled faces and striking dark head-dresses which jutted out over their foreheads in two great horns.

Ginting now rose to speak. I half-straightened my back, hoping that he would use Indonesian, as he knew it so well. But no, Karo was his mother tongue, and again I could not understand anything.

The moaning from the women had been growing louder between the speakers; and as the Revd. Ginting sat down all restraint seemed to go. The widow leant over the dead man's face passionately sobbing. His teenaged daughters grasped his hands, clutching them tightly, as if begging him to come back. Some women attempted to intervene, but it was impossible to stop the torrent of noise and grief.

Tears stung my eyes as I watched. In the prime of life, and gone so quickly! And yet some words kept repeating in my mind, 'We sorrow not as those who have no hope.' We Christians *have* a hope. We *know* we shall see our loved ones again. What had the speakers been saying? Had they been reminding his family of this? Had they no words of comfort? Of course the pain was still there; but for us 'death is swallowed up in victory'.

At some unobtrusive signal, everyone rose to their feet, gathering their belongings. We gathered in a long procession outside on the dusty street. The afternoon sun blazed down with unabated fury, while the flies buzzed sleepily, their siesta disturbed by the crowds of people. I found myself far back in the slow column. Away up ahead the coffin-bearers led the way, surrounded by church leaders and close family. The men and boys followed, leaving the women to come last.

This normally would have been the time for the loudest wailing, as the burial ground was approached; but from far ahead a resolute voice was heard singing. The faithful Bible teacher, who had known so many upheavals in his own life, was leading us all in a Christian hymn. The full-throated slow singing of the Karo believers gathered in volume. Many people in the street turned to stare at this strange funeral procession. The weeping of the family was drowned by hymn after hymn of Christian victory. Yes, the Christians had something their friends did not know. They knew how to be triumphant even in the midst of sorrow.

Sunday came, and with it my official welcome into the Karo church. Martin helped me prepare my speech — my first ever in Indonesian and before a crowd of six or seven hundred! It was just as well I had learned to conquer my fear of public speaking. The opening had to be in the traditional flowery style: 'Brothers and sisters who are loved in the Name of the Lord Jesus Christ, the Saviour and Redeemer of us all . . .' What a mouthful! It took a great deal of learning by heart. One thing we had to make plain was that we were not Dutch, as feelings were still running high. With my fair hair and blue eyes, it was impossible for the people to be certain. My Malay accent must have grated strongly on their ears, but they were very tolerant and most welcoming. My hand nearly dropped off, shaking hands with them all after the service.

'Well, darling, this is the great day. Kabanjahe at last!' Martin rolled out from under the mosquito net and went across to open the shutters. The trace of a breeze which came in from the open window was refreshing. The room grew oppressively hot during the night, but Medan was so notorious for robbery that we all had to sleep with the shutters barred. I stood at the window beside Martin for a moment. The sunlight streamed through the graceful palm-trees and down across the lawn. At this early hour it had not attained its burning strength, but played with a friendly golden gleam on everything it touched. The scent of the gardenia bush under our windows rose to my nostrils. The liquid warbling notes of an oriole floated across the garden. Further away could be heard the sounds of street-vendors calling, and the honk of trishaw hooters as their drivers negotiated the already busy traffic.

'At least we don't have much to pack,' I remarked, starting to get dressed. All our heavy luggage had been sent by sea and we were waiting for news of its arrival at Medan's port. The crossing from Singapore only took a day or two, but ships were not frequent. We had flown over with our sixty-six pounds' air allowance and so were travelling light — though we had added a few things bought in the Medan market. Sybil insisted we should purchase a charcoal stove so that we could manage until our two-burner paraffin cooker, bought in Singapore, arrived. We bought the necessary sack of charcoal, bundle of kindling and boxes of matches to go with it. Two small paraffin lamps, a gallon-sized tin of paraffin, a bucket and a plastic washing-up bowl completed the purchases.

At breakfast Sybil's husband said, 'I'm afraid I can't let you have much money as your Mission allowance has still not come through by post. It's fearfully unreliable these days. I'm pretty low on funds myself,' he went on, glancing at his wallet, 'and with two servants to pay I must keep back enough. Perhaps you can manage on this in the meantime,' and he handed us the equivalent of two pounds.

I looked across at Martin. We were setting up house in a strange town. We had no food stores and no idea what sudden expenses might crop up. And this was all the ready cash we had! There was an embarrassed pause while Sybil's husband added, 'I expect the post will bring your allowance in a day or two. At least it should be through when Martin comes back to pick up the heavy luggage. And the bus fare up to Kabanjahe is not much. I'll pay your trishaw fare to the bus station.'

Just as we were about to leave he had another idea. 'I have six Indonesian Bibles. You may find someone who would like to buy one and that will give you a bit more cash.' Sybil hastily tied the Bibles up into a bundle while two trishaws were called. Martin sat in one and I climbed into the other, while our suit-cases, charcoal, bucket and stove were piled around us. The children all came to say goodbye, the smallest, a little pink-

92

faced cherub, in the arms of his dark-skinned amah. We waved and they all waved back.

'Let us know how you get on! And we'll send you word as soon as your baggage comes through,' they called out, and we were off.

A mixed feeling of excitement and apprehension came over me. What would our 'first ever' home be like? Most people spend so long getting their 'newly-wed' house ready. We knew so little about ours, and had next to nothing for it. Martin told me that the Karo church had two houses in mind. One, which I rather liked the sound of, stood in its own small garden near the church school. It had plenty of water and electricity — both of which were rare commodities in Kabanjahe. The other stood in a row of houses on a busy side-street and would be much more public. But it was this second house which had been chosen, as the drainage for the first one had been found to be insanitary. 'It has two rooms: one upstairs and one down,' Martin informed me. 'There won't be any electricity, but the Church has promised to lay on water.'

We arrived at the bus station and immediately became the centre of a friendly but curious crowd. Our suitcases were exclaimed over — I did not consider them smart, but the onlookers obviously did. Nothing like that could be bought in Medan. Our new charcoal stove was examined. How much had we paid for it? And what a fancy handbag I was carrying; wasn't I afraid of having it snatched? Martin ignored the remarks as he was too busy making sure this was the right bus and seeing that all our stuff was securely tied on the roof. Sacks of rice and baskets of chickens were already up there, but room was made for our luggage too, whilst the bus boys shouted instructions to each other: 'Fix that rope up forward a bit and then throw the end down to me.'

I suddenly became conscious of my gay blue skirt and white blouse and cardigan. They contrasted so sharply with the reds and browns all around me. Most of the Karo women wore clothing dipped in the natural dusky purple dye they made themselves. My snow-white cardigan, which I had thought so suitable for summer wear, was obviously a marvel to them.

93

We climbed into the bus and sat down on two seats near the window. Several of the seats were already taken, the front ones being the first to go. In between tying on the luggage, the bus boys would run up and down shouting, 'Kabanjahe, Kabanjahe!' as if trying to persuade those who were sitting in other buses to change their minds and climb up to the hills with us instead.

'What time will it leave?' I asked Martin.

'Oh, they don't leave to a time-table. They wait until they are full,' he replied.

And the emphasis came on the word 'full', as I was soon to discover. When all the seats were taken, and still more passengers appeared, the bus boys scrambled into the bus again. The passengers knew well what was wanted and meekly stood for a moment while the boys shoved the planks which formed our seats towards the centre of the aisle. The planks now met all the way across, thus making room for more passengers down the middle. The poor people near the window were left with only half a seat to sit on. But was it better to be near the breeze and only have half a seat, or move into the centre? We were feeling so warm by then that we decided to stay put.

After nearly an hour at the bus station we eventually set off. Every inch of space was crowded with people: children sitting on their parents' laps, the bus boys hanging on to the outside of the windows, and a couple of late-comers clinging on to the ladder which led up to the roof at the back.

'This would hardly pass British road-safety laws,' said Martin to me with a twinkle. But it was all so new and exciting there was no time to worry.

We hooted and rattled our way down the streets of Medan, past rows of pretty detached villas still showing a trace of their former Dutch glory, past *kampungs* of the thatched Malay-style houses which had become so familiar to me in Singapore, through an Indian settlement and between rows of Chinese shops until, finally, the bus emerged into the open countryside.

I was intrigued to see that the windows of our bus had no glass, only some torn pieces of canvas which were let down if it was raining. The dust from the road blew into our faces and filled our hair and teeth with grit, but at least the breeze relieved the increasing heat as the sun rose higher and higher.

We drove over flat open countryside, fresh and green with young rice crops and dotted with little thatched houses and clumps of tall coconut palms. At Pancur Batu, where the Revd. Ginting had taken us a few days before, the road crossed over a wide mountain stream filled with giant boulders. The water looked so cool and inviting we longed to get out for a moment, but the driver did not wish to wait long today. After a brief pause for any passengers who wished to get on or off, he started up again.

'Just as well,' I commented, glancing at my watch, 'we don't want to be late arriving.'

Martin smiled teasingly. 'You're still not out of your Singapore ways, are you? They know the buses don't run to time. An hour more or less won't make any difference.' Having already spent six months in Sumatra, he had adjusted radically to the slower pace of life. It had come to be a joke between us while on honeymoon that I finished everything long before he did. Eating, dressing, even just going somewhere — he did everything in slow motion. If we had not laughed at ourselves, it would have been most irritating.

'But you should have heard what Ginting said to me,' said Martin in self defence. 'He saw me walking down the road towards him one day and I thought I was going at quite a normal speed. But he called out, "Don't walk so quickly. They'll think you're a thief!" '

Even with it all explained to me, I still found it hard to slow down. Patience was not one of my virtues.

'Whatever are all those yellow things on the road?' I exclaimed suddenly. 'They look like autumn leaves. No, they're not. Why, they're butterflies! Clouds of little golden butterflies!' It must have been the breeding season as we never saw them again like this. They whirled up in a cloud as the bus rushed through them, swirling in at the windows and sucked out again by the draught. One was caught for a moment against my arm and I marvelled at its fragile beauty. Its gossamer-thin wings gleamed with a golden sheen. The small dark body arched for a moment, and it flew off. We came across other clumps of the same yellow butterflies further up the road. There were hundreds of them out that day.

The road began to climb up the lower foothills. The rice-fields gave way to patches of jungle, with here and there a clearing of sago palms or a crop of maize. The air grew distinctly cooler. No longer did it scorch the inside of one's nostrils: it was now a pleasure to suck it deeply down into one's lungs.

At Bandar Baru, halfway up the high mountainside, the Dutch had built a holiday resort. Pretty dark wood chalets nestled between tall conifers, reminding us of Austria or Switzerland. Here we all climbed out for ten minutes to drink a glass of hot sweet milkless tea in the roadside teashop. It was most welcome after nearly two hours in the bus.

'*Jagung, jagung,*' a woman called to us as we were about to enter our bus again. She was squatting over a charcoal fire by the roadside, briskly fanning the flame which smouldered under a row of corn-on-the-cobs which she was roasting on a grid. They sizzled appetisingly.

'Yes, let's try some. I feel quite hungry,' said Martin, and came back with two piping-hot cobs in his hand. 'Only about threepence each, so I guess we can afford that,' he said. The flavour of the freshly roasted corn was delicious. We munched contentedly as the bus set off once more.

Now the way became very steep. We were climbing steadily, swinging back and forth around hairpin bends as the road snaked upwards. Dense virgin jungle closed in on either side. The tall trees towered above us, their dark green forming an impenetrable mass. Long creepers of deep blue morning-glory swung from their branches.

'Do you think there are tigers in there?' I asked Martin.

'I expect so,' he replied. 'Ginting took me to a remote village called Gunung Meriah shortly before our wedding. They were all talking about tigers there, because we thought we might have to do a seven-mile night march through the jungle in order to catch a bus home. Some of the men didn't want to attempt it, as tigers were known to be in that vicinity. But others thought our flaming torches would be sufficient to keep them at bay.'

'But why ever did you have to walk through the night like that?' I exclaimed.

'Oh, we didn't in the end, because the bus eventually came. You see, there's only one bus goes there once a day and it broke down after it left us there on the Saturday. I had continuous meetings all day Sunday, but had to get up at six the next morning as they said the bus would be there by seven a.m. That weekend I slipped on the way down to the jungle river for a wash and bruised myself all the way up my side and leg. Sitting cross-legged on the floor for hours all day Sunday wasn't much fun. Well, the bus didn't turn up at seven a.m. on Monday and we waited the whole day for it. The local people thought, as it still hadn't come, it must have been needing such drastic repairs that it might not come all week. Of course there was no means of finding out the situation. So we planned our trek through the night in another direction to a different village, which also had a bus once a day leaving at seven a.m. I must say I didn't relish the idea, as I was by then so stiff I could hardly walk. Fortunately, our bus *did* turn up in the end so we were all right.'

We chugged on slowly uphill, the road becoming appreciably more pot-holed. The torrential tropical rain-storms had played havoc with its surface, and often brought the bank down in a minor land-slide, temporarily blocking the way. Fortunately, the last few days had been dry and there were no hold-ups. Now and again, from some vantage point, we caught a glimpse of the distant plains behind us, shimmering in the heat.

'Here's the stone that marks the highest point,' said Martin at last. 'Look back and you should get a good view before we start to cross the plateau.' But the wide expanse, spread out for a moment far behind, was blue with a misty haze and little detail could be made out.

Now we found ourselves in quite a different countryside. The mountain ridge towered above us, while away in front stretched the fertile shelf which was called *Tanah Karo* —

the land of the Karo people. In the cool mountain air of four to five thousand feet we saw crops growing which were familiar in England: fields of huge cabbages, the blue-green of a thick crop of leeks, the gleaming scarlet of a field of ripening tomatoes, and the feathery tufts of carrot-tops. In spite of the mid-day sun, I buttoned up my cardigan. I had shed it earlier when we passed through the hot plains, but the air was deliciously cool here. Two majestic volcanoes stood out against the skyline: Sebayak, rugged and sprawling closer by, and Sinabung, shaped like a perfect pyramid in the distance, with one long white gash down the near-side. Puffs of steam formed an everchanging cloud above each one.

'Isn't it magnificent!' I exclaimed excitedly. 'I do hope we'll manage to climb one of them sometime.'

'See the smoke?' asked Martin. 'The Karos say if there's smoke coming out steadily they're quite safe. The pressure is being released all the time. But if it stops, you'd better look out, as it may be building up for an eruption. They're not too safe to climb,' he added. 'High winds sweep down those ravines. But there's sure to be someone who would be willing to be our guide.'

'Kabanjahe!' the bus boy suddenly called. At last we were there.

'We'd like to go to Christian Street,' Martin said to him.

'Will it take us to the house?' I asked surprised.

'Oh, yes. If you've come all this way, you can expect them to take you to your door. You wait; we may circle all round the town first, dropping people off at different places. There's no set route.'

The driver decided to set us down first, and soon turned into a dusty side-street just off the market. A row of shop-like houses lined one side and a barbed-wire fence, cutting off someone's vegetable garden, marked the other.

'This is it!' announced Martin. 'Look, there's the Church Office,' he said pointing to the vegetable garden. 'These houses were built by the Church. That's why they named it Christian Street. That one belongs to Rachel, the Bible woman, and this one next to ours to the Revd. Bukit.'

We ground to a halt. The bus boy scrambled up the roof ladder to lift our bags down, and Martin went round to check that everything was there. I gazed across at our home to see what it was like. The whole street was a continuous row of simple wooden houses, opening straight on to the road. The upstairs rooms projected outwards, forming a covering over the pavement, and were supported by a line of concrete pillars. The front of each house was formed by wooden planks which could be completely removed in the daytime so as to make the 'shop' easily accessible to the street. They were all painted in the same yellow and green.

Several people emerged from number 61. They had been busy cleaning it for us and getting it ready.

'Welcome, welcome!' they reiterated warmly, shaking us by the hand and helping us carry our things inside. 'We're so glad you've come! We want to welcome you to Karoland. Did you have an easy journey on the bus? How do you like your new home?'

We gazed around us. They had spread a large rush mat on the centre of the plain cement floor for us to sit on. (We later discovered that this was only on loan for the day.) At the other end stood a rectangular dining-table and six upright chairs, together with one cupboard. Nothing else. But the walls were freshly whitewashed and everything looked clean and nice.

'It's lovely,' we said.

'You must see upstairs too,' they insisted, leading the way through the door at the far end. This led into the back premises, semi-open to the elements, with the staircase leading steeply up. Beyond was a tiny wash-room, containing a small water-butt and tap, and a primitive toilet consisting of a deep hole in the ground with a cement surround to squat on. Upstairs they had partitioned a corner of the room near the window as our bedroom. They must have placed the iron-framed three-foot-ten-inch bed in it before building the partition, as it could never have got through the narrow door. The bed had an extra rail around it to prevent the kapok mattress spreading. And as Martin had to concertina his long legs up to fit in it, he found the rail a particular nuisance. But we did not know that then, and everything looked fine. Another table stood near the window 'for Martin to study at' and this completed the furniture. Altogether the house was clean and roomy. We were delighted with it.

'Now we'll all go downstairs and have some tea,' said one of the Karo women, who had obviously placed herself in charge. I looked at her round motherly face and twinkling eyes and could see that she was used to organising things. She had introduced herself to us by saying: 'My eldest child is called Pesta.'

I wanted to ask, 'But what's *your* name?' only fortunately something held my tongue. We were kept several times from making some awful mistake during those first few days. We later discovered that you never call anyone by their own name, but only as mother or father of their eldest child. Even Christians did this, although it stemmed from the old animistic fear that the spirits might find out one's name and so be able to harm one.

Mother of Pesta organised us all downstairs and had Rachel, the young Bible woman, bring in the tea. We sat down on the rush mat, but she obviously disapproved of the way my feet and ankles could not tuck under my skirt.

'Rasmita, run and fetch a sarong,' she ordered one of the pretty teenage girls. And when it was brought she made me step into the long length of material, sewn into a circle by stitching the ends together. Rapidly she pleated it securely round my waist so that it would hang down to my ankles.

'There. That's better,' she said. 'Now you can sit properly.'

While we all drank tea Mother of Pesta went out to the back to examine our luggage.

'What are you going to eat for lunch?' she demanded a little sharply when she came back.

'Well, there's an eating-shop round the corner,' Martin began.

'Nonsense,' she cut in. 'We can't hear of that. Rachel, off you go and get them something hot. Have you got a food carrier to bring it back in? Make sure it's something really tasty.'

100

Again we were saved! I had not wanted to trouble to light our charcoal stove to cook the lunch, so we had decided to eat out, not realising what an offence this could cause. We had come to live among these people as their guests and they could not possibly allow us to go out to buy our first meal. Of course, it saved us a good deal of money too as we were so short of ready cash!

I half wondered about unpacking, but by Karo standards visitors were not to be left alone. Mother of Pesta, Rasmita and the others stayed talking until Rachel finally appeared with a delicious hot curry and some boiled rice. She brought enamel plates with her from her own house, and some spoons and forks in case we did not wish to eat with our fingers.

'Good!' commented Mother of Pesta, examining each dish. 'Now you have a good lunch and we'll leave you to it. But we'll be back around three o'clock because they are going to have a welcome here for you.'

She picked up her dark purple shawl and wrapped it round her shoulders. 'Come on, girls, get your shoes on,' she said to the others, slipping her bare brown feet into a pair of sandals by the door. Her plump comfortable figure blocked the light from the doorway for a moment as she turned and said, 'Have a good look round and tell us if there is anything you need. I can send Pesta round with it.'

Martin and I looked happily at each other as they left.

'Isn't it wonderful to feel *wanted*?' I remarked. 'Just think of some of our missionaries putting up with suspicion and hostility when they go to a new place. What a contrast this is!'

Chapter Nine

Karoland

WE FELT THE warm glow of the Karo welcome for many days. Each church group wished to do something special for us.

'The elders and deacons want to hold a welcome-meeting in your home tonight,' we were told one morning. We had no idea what to expect, but everything was taken out of our hands. As it grew dusk and people wended their way home from the fields for an evening meal, Rasmita appeared at the door. Her family lived in a far-off village but she was staying with Rachel, who appeared to run a small hostel for teenage girls. Buxom and dimpled, Rasmita had lovely long dark hair which hung to her waist.

'Do you have any rush mats?' she asked with a friendly smile.

'Well, no, we don't,' I replied, 'except that little one.' I pointed to a small one we had been given as a wedding present by some Malay friends.

'Oh, *that* won't do!' Rasmita exclaimed. 'I'll go and borrow some.'

Just as we were finishing our supper she came back, carrying an enormous roll over her sturdy shoulder. Rachel and another friend followed with two more mats. They pushed our dining-chairs back against the wall and unrolled the long six-foot-wide strips of matting to cover the floor. We brought in our two small paraffin lamps, as by now it was getting quite dark. When Rachel saw how inadequate they were she disappeared. Suddenly a blaze of light entered the room. It came from a pressure lamp carried by a little old man dressed in a faded grey open-neck shirt and a rather dingy purple sarong. He set it down in the centre of the floor and came over to shake hands warmly.

'I'm Father of Contoh,' he said, grasping Martin's big white hands in his own gnarled brown ones. 'I live just opposite you, down the road a bit. Welcome to Karoland.'

He stayed chatting while the girls continued preparations for the gathering. 'I've not been a Christian for so very long,' he said in answer to Martin's questions. 'Perhaps five years. But it has made such a difference. I never used to do any work before then — just sat around talking with the other men in the coffee-shops. I really hadn't any purpose in life. Now I help Mother of Contoh work the fields. Mind you, I can't dig like she can,' he added with a toothless smile. 'She's been brought up to do it from girlhood.'

One by one the elders and deacons began to gather. Martin and I were told to sit on the mat at the far end of the room opposite the door, as host and hostess. Each guest slipped his shoes off and came across to shake hands. The men then sat down on one side and the few women on the other. A sturdy little round-faced man, with a snub nose and greying hair came in.

'That's the Archbishop,' whispered Martin to me. I looked up surprised. He was wearing dark baggy trousers and a dingy open-neck shirt, which might have been white once. He carried his sarong loosely over one shoulder. 'Yes, that's the Revd. Si Tepu,' went on Martin, 'you know, the head of all the Karo Church.' Si Tepu greeted us both and sat down in the place of honour at Martin's right hand. I sensed he was eyeing me, and wondered what he was thinking. 'Was I sitting properly, with my legs tucked into my borrowed sarong?' I asked myself. Perhaps he did not approve of my fair hair which made me look so very like the Dutch. I had grown it long specially, as Martin had written to say that all Indonesian women have long hair. It was tucked into a smooth French roll at the back. But I need not have worried. Although the Revd. Si Tepu appeared a trifle brusque, underneath he was friendly. And naturally he was slightly on the defensive: he had been head of the Church for some time now: he did not wish the new missionaries to usurp his position!

We sang several hymns interspersed with long speeches of

welcome. Martin replied at length on our behalf and included a short message from the Bible. I hesitatingly added a few words, feeling desperately the inadequacy of my language. I had been learning Malay for less than a year and now had to make a drastic dialect switch. Fortunately Indonesian was a second language to our Karo friends, so they were not as critical as they might have been if they had spoken it from childhood. At least they did not show it.

Finally Rachel, who had made herself at home with my charcoal stove, appeared with steaming hot tea for us all. This was the sign for the gifts to be produced. We never ceased to marvel at the generosity of the Karo people. They knew we had no rice-fields of our own, and for them rice is the staff of life. Wherever we went we were laden with gifts, so that during our two years in Karoland, although we ate rice two or three times a day, we never bought a single grain. We even had plenty to share with Sybil and her family in Medan.

Tonight was our first taste of this generosity. Mother of Pesta, who, we now realised, was a Church elder, produced a bulging plaited bag from under her shawl. She hitched up her sarong and stepped over to place the gift in front of me. Each of the women in turn did the same, and then the men passed the gifts from their wives forward. Rasmita was hastily sent to find some larger rice containers, and the streams of long white grains filled bag after bag. Some had placed a few eggs on top of theirs; others a money gift. They could not possibly have guessed how short we were of ready cash. What a difference these gifts would make until our money came through!

During the evening Martin happened to mention that he had six Indonesian Bibles. Bibles for sale! Several elders' eyes lit up. How much were they? Did we have any other Christian books?

'Well, we can get some when we next go down to Medan.'

So, in a most inconspicuous way, our literature work started. Martin had been told in Medan, 'It's no use taking books up to Kabanjahe. Nobody reads anything up there.' But we were to discover how wrong this was. And we have found this again and again, even in Britain. Present people with attractive, helpful Christian books and they will sell like hot cakes!

Our immediate financial problems were solved by the gifts of money we received and by those first Bibles. The price of two Bibles proved sufficient to pay Martin's bus fare back to Medan the following week. He stocked up with a good variety of more Bibles, children's books, biographies, study aids, and anything else he could find. I stood two large cartons, one on top of the other, near our open front door. We covered them with a table cloth and spread the books out on display.

After a short time more cartons had to be found and a larger cloth, as our 'bookshop' extended its scope. In the months to come we found we were selling more and more literature in answer to a tremendous hunger for Christian books, and we had enough ready cash from the sales not to need money transferred any longer from Jakarta.

It took us some time to appreciate the value of our new financial footing. During our stay in Indonesia there was roaring inflation. It was a particularly difficult time economically for the whole country. A few years later, when President Suharto came to power, things were to improve radically, but during the early 1960s prices shot up beyond all control.

Martin's first letter to his mother after we both arrived in Medan said,

We have no bread or flour here at all now. Paraffin has risen by 500% in price, meat by 50%, travel by 100% on top of the 50% rise just before I went to Singapore. Rice rose 100% in my first six months here.

And another letter two months later said,

Fares have just gone up again and are now just over 300% higher than when I went to Singapore for our wedding. In fact all prices are going up and up at an alarming rate – it's very hard indeed on people here. We have just been told that there is a plan for the Government to take over distribution and sale of all major articles in order to assure a fair distribution to all.

A much-coveted government permit the week before enabled us to buy a tin of paraffin for twenty-five p. instead of the ordinary market rate of three pounds! Martin continued:

Most people now use fire-wood, but even that is very expensive, and many are reduced to burning rice-chaff in spite of the fearful smoke and smell it gives off!

With the value of money depreciating at such an alarming rate, any money-order posted to us from our Mission headquarters in Jakarta would have lost value appreciably during its three weeks in transit by post. Also, as a Missionary Society, our money came into the country as U.S. dollars and the rate of exchange was fixed by the Government. When Martin first went to Medan we received 45 rupiahs to the U.S. dollar. Six months later when I joined him, we received 70, and within another three months this rose to 150. But this lagged far behind the black-market rate of 900 to 1,000 rupiahs per U.S. dollar, which was what the purchasing value of the money really was.

The situation deteriorated so drastically that no one wished to have money on their hands. All cash was immediately turned into staple commodities — rice, sugar, cloth, anything that would hold its value. Shops stocking more expensive goods were reluctant to carry on business at all. They valued their articles at more than the price they could ask. Martin told me whimsically of a sign he noticed in a furniture shop in Medan:

We are willing to sell some of our stock today.

Now Martin and I began to see how God had provided a way for us to cope in such uncertain economic conditions. By ordering Christian books from Jakarta, we too were handling a

107

commodity, not money. They were printed in Indonesia and so were not linked to any artificial foreign-exchange rate. When they arrived we could put up the prices in line with the inflation of other goods. And they met with such a good sale that they provided the steady stream of cash we needed for day-to-day living.

One day, when we had been in our new home about two weeks, the Medan bus lurched to a halt outside our front door and the bus boy ran over with a letter from Sybil's husband. To pay a bus boy was by far the most reliable way of sending news to us, as letters could take at least a week from Medan, and some never arrived.

Martin called out to where I was cooking on the low table under the back stairs.

'Our heavy luggage has come! I'll go down tomorrow and try to make arrangements to bring it up.'

'Oh, won't that be good!' I exclaimed, red-faced from trying to blow the charcoal into a better glow. 'We'll be able to cook by paraffin, and we'll have the lovely bright Aladdin lamp I bought you — and all our beautiful wedding presents! Won't it be fun making everything look really nice!'

The charcoal stove had become my *bête noir*. With our back premises semi-open, the bag of charcoal was now damp and extremely difficult to light. It was impossible to keep the fire in all the time, so I decided to set it going only once a day. For breakfast we bought a large thermos of black tea from the coffee-shop on the corner. They would even give us boiling water free of charge with which we could mix some of our precious Nescafé, but we had not the face to ask for it too often! I lit the stove mid-morning and cooked enough food to last us two meals. What was left over we ate cold in the evening. Yes, it would be good to have a paraffin cooker which would light easily with just one match!

The next day, Martin caught the six a.m. bus down to Medan, but he did not reappear until long after dark. I was beginning to wonder what had happened. He had taken another bus a further fifteen miles to the port of Belawan. Here five hours were spent, in the fearful heat, going from office to office to establish that he was the owner of the cases, and to obtain permission to take them away. All the time he was wondering how he would get them up to Kabanjahe. It would be a fearful job hoisting them all on to the roof of the Belawan-to-Medan bus. Then he would have somehow to cross the city to the further bus station and finally pile them all on to the bus to Kabanjahe. He prayed hard as he trudged around the stifling docks.

Again the Lord had it all planned. Hot and sticky, but triumphantly holding the precious permit to remove our luggage, Martin sat down on the little wooden stool of a coffee-shop and ordered a refreshing glass of tea. He was inwardly praising the Lord because all the luggage had come through safely with no customs to pay. As he was drinking he looked around him and suddenly noticed the word KABANJAHE printed in large letters on the side of a vegetable-lorry. Heavy crates of cabbages were being heaved from the back and dumped on the quay-side. They were obviously due to be shipped to some other country, perhaps Singapore, he thought with a smile.

Then his smile grew even wider. The lorry would surely return to Kabanjahe for another load. They would not want to go back empty-handed. Perhaps he could persuade them to take our boxes! He watched them finish the unloading as he downed his last drops of sweet, strong tea. Timing his arrival carefully, he strolled over to speak to the driver. Yes, he would be glad to take the stuff, and Martin could ride in the back too. How easily it all worked out in the end!

We saw God's hand on us that day in another way. Arriving as they did after dark, we were able to unload the boxes with the minimum of curious onlookers. It was not that we had anything to hide, but by now we realised how ostentatious some of our Western goods appeared. We decided to keep all our nice things upstairs and to make that into a room where we could relax and enjoy ourselves. Downstairs, where visitors were free to come in and out, we kept as simple as possible.

During the next few days Martin discovered hidden talents.

He had never enjoyed making things with his hands, but he turned the crates in which our two bicycles had travelled into a large kitchen cupboard for me. 'It's not a thing of beauty, but its door works a treat!' he wrote home proudly. I seem to remember that we had to tilt it backwards with small wooden wedges underneath to prevent the door swinging open all the time! However, it certainly was useful.

On Martin's next visit to Medan he splashed out and bought us two simple cane chairs and a small table, so that we at least had something comfortable to sit on. Up to then we had placed four of our upright chairs near the door, grouped around a cardboard box covered with a cloth. Here we served drinks to the constant stream of visitors.

I cut up the curtain material, which Mary and I had bought in Singapore, to screen off a small guest-room upstairs. Here we set up our camp bed. A wooden tray on top of another cardboard box served as a bedside table. We felt ready for overnight guests now. Two wooden boxes covered by gay chintz formed the bedside table in our room, while two larger crates were used as cupboard space. Placed at an angle and covered with Martin's dark green bedspread, they gave a lovely 'sideboard' effect for displaying our ornaments. The downstairs wall we brightened by pinning up gay tea-towels showing London scenes. The comment from visitors was not on the Horse Guards, or Buckingham Palace, but 'what wonderful drawing pins those are! They don't bend when you stick them into wood.'

The shining brass tap in the back premises proved rather a let-down. Sticking to the letter of their agreement, the Church had installed a brand new tap; but it was no guarantee that any water would come through it!

On our first morning in the new home I stood at the top of our wooden stairs and called over to our neighbour. As the backs of the houses were separated only by low walls, one could get a good view of all the neighbours' cooking-premises from up there.

'The water has stopped flowing this morning! What's happened? Why isn't any coming through?'

Young Revd. Bukit, newly ordained and just about to get married, climbed to the top of his stairs and spoke to me across the narrow space of our kitchen.

'Oh, we all turned off our taps yesterday so that your water butt would fill up,' he remarked casually. 'But we can't do it every day. Just leave your tap on all the time and you'll probably get a trickle morning and evening.'

We soon learned the value of a heavy shower of rain to supplement our meagre water supply. 'It's raining!' we used to groan in England, eyeing the grey skies despondently. 'It's raining!' we would now call out excitedly, and would both rush to collect the galvanised buckets and join the neighbours outside on our covered pavement. Someone had slashed the pipe which led from the guttering on the roof. Its broken end hung next to the pillar supporting our upstairs room. As the rain increased in strength water started to flow out of the jagged opening.

'Don't catch that first water,' the Revd. Bukit remonstrated, laughing. 'It's too dirty!' Wait until the roof has washed clean.'

So we were initiated into the art of coping with the water shortage. With buckets brim-full of lovely clean rain water, we would race through our downstairs room and empty them into the water-tub at the back. Then we would toss off our shoes and Martin would roll up his trousers to prevent them getting soaking wet. Splashing and laughing we would hurry back and forth until every water-container we owned was filled. Then I would set to and scrub the downstairs cement floor right through, in gay abandonment because for once there was plenty of water to spare.

Those floors needed a regular scrubbing as otherwise I could not get a good night's sleep. The connecting factor was fleas! Quite unavoidable I always managed to pick up a few of these unwelcome passengers each time I went to the market. It was a help when I learnt to examine my legs and skirt just before stepping into the front door. But the little blighters had an unaccountable fascination for me and a few could easily get missed. Our visitors probably added to their numbers even if

111

they were not aware of the present they brought us. It all added up to a constant battle. If I let down my vigilance for a few days, woe betide my tender skin and my beauty-sleep!

But there were worse things to worry about than mere fleas. The cholera which had greeted us within our first week was now rampant through North Sumatra. People were being brought in to the small overcrowded Kabanjahe hospital and dying on the way. The one doctor there was desperately over-worked and, with most inadequate facilities, most of his cholera patients died.

'Have you all had anti-cholera inoculations?' we urged our new-found friends. The queues for the vaccine took hours to be dealt with, but many of the church people went. Their report was a little discouraging.

'They say this injection won't guarantee our not getting it; but if we do, at least we won't die!' We were thankful that we had been given good vaccine shots in Singapore! 'Well, make sure you only drink boiled water and leave off all uncooked fruit and vegetables for the time being,' was all we could say.

The hospital contended against tremendous odds. Built by the Dutch missionaries, the Church looked upon it as their own property when the Dutch were driven out. But the Karo Church had neither the man-power nor the resources to run it, so the Government took it over. As few doctors were willing to stay for long in our remote mountain market-town, the turnover in personnel was rapid. The hospital suffered from the same water-shortage as the rest of the town. The nurses were lucky if the floors of the wards could be washed once a week. The bed-linen was grey and soiled, the feverish patients perspiring and smelly. The whole place stank. Many of the local people preferred to be ill at home, and even die, rather than go there.

Not only was there the problem of health but also the econ-omic situation at that time made the cost of living rise alarmingly. Those on government pay, such as nurses and teachers, were particularly badly hit. Their salaries were fixed, and trailed far behind the rising prices. Yet if they resigned and

112

took a different job they knew they would never be employed by the Government again. Many teachers took posts in two schools at once, and no one was surprised if they failed to put in an appearance when they should have been teaching.

'Oh, he's over at his other school,' they would explain with a shrug of the shoulders.

'What are you doing, Rachel?' I called out of the front window to her one morning. I was making our bed after breakfast and could see her bobbing up and down across the narrow street, working on the other side of the barbed-wire fence in the grounds of the church office. She straightened her slim, lithe body for a moment and called up,

'Hoeing!'

'Are you planting out some flowers?' I asked.

Rasmita, who was working with her, pulled up another handful of weeds with a laugh, and called out,

'Of course not! We're putting in corn and tubers. We must have something to eat.'

It was the same all over the area. Every bit of waste land and even the gardens were being dug up to grow vegetables. If it had not been for the rich, fertile soil, food would have been desperately short. We had news that famine was spreading on the over-crowded island of Java. In a letter home we wrote:

It is now cheaper to get all foods except vegetables and fruit by air freight from Penang, even with the 30 per cent duty to pay and the cost of transport.

Martin had lost twenty-five pounds in weight during his first six months in Indonesia. He had always been tall and thin, but he was down to eight stone six pounds at our wedding! During our honeymoon he put on a stone, and I was determined that he should not lose it again. News of missionary friends of ours in Jakarta stressed how important it was to keep fit and not to overwork. While on their honeymoon the bride had contracted infective hepatitis and had gone into a coma. When at last she came round she had no memory of the wedding or even of her husband! Yet how could we keep fit and eat well in such a

113

situation, with shortages on every hand? God knew our needs, and again and again provided accordingly. Gifts of eggs and rice were constantly lavished upon us. The women who sold bananas in the market were all Christians and would vie with one another to present us with a bunch. Dear thin little wrinkled Mother of Contoh (wife of the old man who had lent us his good pressure lamp), grew watercress and a particularly tasty green vegetable. She thrust great bunches of them into my hands whenever I went to market. And when, from sheer embarrassment at her generosity, I took another path for several days, she called at our home with an even bigger bunch saying emphatically, 'You've been avoiding me! I know you have! You must take these.'

'See that old cow?' Martin asked me one morning as we were clearing up the breakfast things. I looked out the front door and saw a scraggy humped-back specimen being led past by a slip of a boy.

'Know where it's going?'

I shook my head.

'That's our meat for today!' he announced teasingly. I soon learned to time my marketing perfectly. Talk about fresh meat — we certainly had it! One had to turn a blind eye to the fact that it was still twitching. If you left it any longer the flies would be all over it. To my joy I discovered that, apart from the bony bits, it was all the same price. So out came my college notes to remind me where the best cuts were on a carcass, and I would point to the most tender portion of rump steak and ask for it to be cut off there! We found we were living in the only town in Karoland which had fresh meat every day. As we had no refrigerator this made a tremendous difference.

My college study of dietetics helped us to understand how to maintain a good balanced diet, even with very limited and, to us, 'strange' foodstuffs. We marvelled again at how God knew and cared about every need of ours. We learnt to eat mainly local food, and I would often have long chats in the market, asking the women how to cook some unfamiliar item they were offering for sale.

For a while we sent in a monthly order to Penang.

Margarine, jam, dried milk, tinned meats and cheese all helped to add variety to our diet. Sybil's husband collected both their order and ours at the airport, paying the customs duty and airfreight. Martin would plan a visit to Medan a few days later to pick up the parcels and see to any other business he had in the city. One evening after he had returned from such a visit I noticed a strange smell.

'There must be a dead rat, or something. Can't you smell it?' I asked. But he noticed nothing, so after some minutes' futile searching I sat down again.

When we went up to bed the smell grew more pronounced, 'Surely you can smell something!' I expostulated. 'Has one of the stray cats crawled in here to die?'

This time, Martin caught a whiff of it too. Holding the feeble paraffin lamp in one hand, he started to search the up-stairs room, sniffing loudly as he went. I felt for the torch which always lay by our bed and began at the other end. Finally we met at the food-parcels which had been deposited in a corner.

'It's the parcels!' I exclaimed. 'There's something funny about them!' I held the lamp aloft while Martin hastily undid them. The smell suddenly became overpowering. Holding my nose I rushed for the door, forgetting in my haste that I still held the lamp and so plunged Martin into darkness. Breathing in great gulps of fresh air, I gasped, 'Whatever is it?'

'How can I tell in the dark?' came his voice from the gloomy interior. 'Smells like bad fish. Bring the lamp and we'll see.' Taking another deep breath, I plucked up my courage and went back. Two once-fresh herrings, wrapped in grease-proof paper, lay on top. They had sweltered through two days' wait at a hot airport, another couple of days lying around the Medan home, and then a long bus journey up to us.

'Goodness – I ordered tinned herrings in tomato sauce,' I managed to stammer. 'Quick, take them out and bury them before the neighbours come round to see what we are up to!'

We stole across to the public rubbish tip at the end of our

road. Digging a hole as best we could with a broken stick and a piece of old metal lying around, we buried the herrings as deeply as possible!

Chapter Ten

The Karo Church

WITHIN A WEEK of moving up to our new home the 'Archbishop', as Martin jokingly called him, came to visit us. He sat down rather stiffly on one of the upright chairs near the door, while I hurried off to make him some tea. The Revd. Sitepu was dressed in a faded old jacket and the usual baggy trousers. He fingered his topee lovingly, and slowly removed it. He and his topee were inseparable, as we were to notice. We often wondered if some Dutch pastor had given it to him many years before, and if he kept it for old times' sake. Certainly no one else ever wore one — except one other elderly Bible teacher.

When I came back with the tea, Martin was trying to set him at ease by asking about his family. Whether it was the Revd. Sitepu that was not really at home in the Indonesian language, or whether he was shy of these strange foreigners we did not know, but we never managed to become really close with him during our time in Kabanjahe.

'Would you like to go to a wedding?' he asked us rather abruptly.

My eyes lit up. 'O yes, that would be interesting!'

'I'm going to one today,' he announced. 'I'll be back in about half an hour. See you then!'

Hastily he swallowed his tea and excused himself.

I looked at Martin when he was gone: 'Half an hour!' I exclaimed. 'What shall I wear? What shall we take for a present? Who is it, anyway?'

'You're in Indonesia now, not Singapore,' he teased. 'You look fine as you are. And they won't expect a present except from their close relations. There will probably be 500 or 600 guests. It's they who have to feed us.'

Some while later there was the honk of a jeep at our door. I grabbed a cardigan in case it turned cold, and we both went out. The Revd. Sitepu was sitting at the wheel, his topee stuck rather jauntily on the back of his head. The Karo Church owned two jeeps, one of which was used by the Revd. Ginting in Medan and the other the Revd. Sitepu kept for his own use. This one was, if anything, in an even more dilapidated condition than the other. We climbed in the back and greeted the two other passengers there. Sitepu stopped to pick up three or four more people in different parts of Kabanjahe before finally setting off down the main road which led towards Medan.

Going along, Martin chatted with the other men while I tried to catch a peep of the view through the canvas doorway at the back. A swarm of flies steadily made their way inside, trapped by the overhanging awning. They crawled over our faces and clothes while I tried in vain to keep them off.

'There are always flies near Brastagi,' our friendly hosts explained. 'They are attracted by the fish manure they spread on the fields.' Seeing my futile attempts at driving them off, one of them went on, 'they're quite clean. You don't need to worry.' 'Clean flies. An interesting new species,' I thought. Martin found on a return Sunday visit how bad they could be. It was impossible to read the pages of his Bible while he was preaching unless he kept his other hand constantly waving back and forth across it. But our Karo friends did not seem to mind the flies; so unless they actually walked across my face I tried not to notice them.

We stopped at Brastagi to pick up the Bible teacher, all of us crowding up just that little bit more to make room for him. There seemed no limit to the number of passengers Sitepu was prepared to cram on board. We only hoped the old, spluttering engine would stand the strain. The Bible teacher lived in a little white wooden house at the entrance of the wide Brastagi High Street.

'This used to be a Dutch pleasure resort,' Martin explained to me. 'Can you see those villas set back in the hills around? That's where they would stay for their holiday. We must come here when we have a free day.'

118

Continuing along the main road for several miles, Sitepu suddenly swung off on to a cart track. I clasped one of the roof supports as we lurched and jolted along. It was lovely countryside, but we could only catch a glimpse of it as we rattled past. In one of the fields were three women, their backs bending and straightening in rhythm as they hoed between their rows of carrots. One had a baby strapped on her back with a long piece of purple cloth. On this side stood a field of tall ripening maize, and there a splash of red by the roadside betrayed a wild poinsettia bush. A bank of white Queen Anne's lace and bright yellow daisies flashed past against the green. Our progress was slower here, as the cart-track almost petered out in places. Then it bravely took shape again and we pressed on. Finally, we came to the village of Bukit, and all climbed out of the jeep, glad to stretch our cramped limbs. We were told that the wedding procession had already gone on to the church, so we hurried off to join it.

The church looked as if it had been transplanted straight out of a child's model village, with its wooden walls, gabled roof, and high pointed spire. It was crowded with people but places were found for us, and Sitepu started the wedding ceremony. Even before looking at the bridal couple my eye was caught by the massed flowers which filled the front of the church. Luxuriant gladioli of every shade and colour displayed their beauty in tall portable baskets.

The bride replied to Sitepu's questions in a barely audible whisper. Her dark head was bent low and her eyes were fixed on the floor: she was clearly very nervous. The rich sarong she wore, embossed with gold thread, gleamed with her slightest movement. The groom, dressed in a smart western-style suit, answered with more assurance.

After the wedding ceremony the congregation formed into a long procession to escort the bridal couple to the reception. We wound slowly through the village, giving me a chance to have my first close-up of the picturesque Karo houses. They towered above us on either side, each one built to house eight families and constructed without a single nail. The huge stilts which supported them were made of roughly hewn logs. High above rose the magnificent black roofs of dark sago-fibre thatch, sweeping in strong lines towards the sky. The junction of the gables was filled with a gay intricate pattern of woven bamboo, painted scarlet, blue and yellow. To crown it all, a pair of large buffalo horns graced the point of the gable at either end.

'They look even more striking in the moonlight,' Martin remarked to me. 'Imagine those black towering curves against a brilliant moonlit sky.'

We reached an open field where preparations had been going on all morning. Round the edge shady arcades had been erected, using small trees and palm fronds. Here we all sat down to wait while the meal was cooked. Great cauldrons of rice steamed in the centre of the field and a roughly dissected pig simmered slowly over another enormous fire. A group of gaily-dressed girls spread out the piles of enamel plates ready for the food to be served.

'Look! Those must be the wedding presents!' I pointed to some new arrivals. All the guests had brought a gift of money as they entered the field, but the close family was expected to provide the couple with their household furniture. And here it all came: a new tightly rolled mattress on the shoulders of a staggering man; pillows with heavily embroidered pillow slips; large rush mats to spread on the floor; even the new cupboard was carried out and placed near the bridal couple for all to see.

We gossiped and chatted an hour or more until at last the food was served. It was no mean task to cater for five or six hundred people. But we were not to eat in peace. Sitepu suddenly appeared.

'I think it's going to rain,' he said, hastily glancing at the darkening sky. 'We must leave at once or my jeep will get stuck in the mud on that bad road.' Quickly swallowing a few mouthfuls of lunch, we said our farewells and scrambled into the jeep. Was it my imagination or were we now more crowded than ever before? Certainly there seemed less room. My knees bumped those of the man opposite, and someone else's elbow jutted into my back. But there was no time to complain as the little old jeep lurched and jumped over the uneven cart-track and the sky grew rapidly darker. Huge drops of rain began to spatter the canvas roof and almost simultaneously a flash of lightning split the sky.

'Faster, Sitepu!' one of the men called out, trying desperately to keep his seat as we hurtled round a corner.

'The rain's coming in on you,' another shouted to his friend as the torrential downpour gathered pace.

What with trying to hold the torn pieces of the canvas roof together, and clinging tightly so as not to be thrown on to the lap of the person opposite, we were a laughing, shouting mob. The valiant old jeep raced on as best it could through the streams which were beginning to flow down the roadway, on and on until it reached the main road. Then, as if it had accomplished all that could be expected, the engine spluttered a couple of times and died!

'I can't go any further,' Sitepu shouted to us from the front. 'We'll have to catch a bus home.'

We found a derelict house by the roadside which afforded us some shelter, and waited hopefully for something to come from the Medan direction.

While sitting there Sitepu leant over to Martin. 'I've taken you to a *kampung* (village) today,' he said, 'but I don't want you to go to one on your own. The memory of the Dutch war is too fresh in many people's minds. They might mistake your nationality and I can't be responsible for your safety.'

We found this warning hard to stick to as the weeks went by. Our days were full and busy, but once our heavy luggage had arrived and the house was straight at last, we both felt like a day off.

'Tell you what,' suggested Martin. 'Let's cycle to *kampung* Lingga. It's not far. Ginting took me once before, so the people know me. Everyone's so friendly here in Kabanjahe I can't believe we'd come to any harm. There are lots of the lovely eight-family houses there.'

So we set off together on our bicycles down a new road I had not travelled before, passing first of all the old pump-house which gave the town its water-supply.

'Pity they can't install a better one,' commented Martin over his shoulder as we swung up the hill the other side. 'Still, I suppose we shouldn't grumble at our hour's trickle morning and evening. It seems to be just about enough.'

Three-quarters of an hour later we cycled into Lingga and propped our bicycles against a tree. The eight-family houses here were even more striking than those at Bukit. We wandered around the *kampung* for a while giving a cheery good-morning to the few people we met and feeling relieved at their smiling retort. There were no roads in these *kampungs* — just the well-trampled paths of bare earth which wriggled between the massive houses. I noticed that not all the houses were the same size: smaller ones stood in between, balanced on even taller stilts, and with only a tiny door near the roof.

'Those are where they store their rice,' Martin pointed out. 'They take the ladder away so that no one else can steal it while they are working in the fields. And look over there. That's the boys' hostel.' He indicated another house different in style from the main ones and reached only by a long ladder.

'What do you mean, the boys' hostel?' I asked surprised.

'When the boys reach their teens they move out from the eight-family homes and all sleep together over there. It's sensible in a way, but they can feel very cut off from their parents. They stay there until they get married.'

We stopped for a moment to watch some women pounding the husks off rice. They were working in a long, low building with an unusually elaborate roof. The house had no walls, so we could easily see inside. Huge tree-trunks lay along the length of the floor with numerous bowl-shaped hollows scooped out of them. Here the women placed their unhusked rice and pounded it steadily with the ends of heavy poles. A tiny dark-haired baby was strapped securely on one of the women's backs. Fast asleep, he appeared quite unconcerned at the way he was being jogged up and down.

A little further on we came to a house much grander than all the others.

'Ginting told me one of the kings of Karoland lived here,' Martin said. 'He was killed during the war for independence. There used to be five kings, but the one who lived in Lingga was the chief. See this beautiful engraving they have made around the walls of his house, and that extra fancy bit on the roof.'

By this time we were hot and tired, and one of us suggested a drink. Not knowing the Karo custom that only men enter the coffee-houses, we both went in and Martin asked for two glasses of sweet tea. The man behind the counter stared at us rather curiously, but obligingly brought what we asked for.

'You needn't worry,' said Martin smiling; 'we're not Dutch. We're English. We've come to live in Kabanjahe. Your Karo Church invited us.'

Some of the men at the other tables gathered round. They were all tough, farming folk and many carried the usual sharp *parang* (knife) hanging from their belts. But we had no cause for alarm. They were friendly and plied us with questions. How long had we been in Karoland? What were we doing here? How many children had we? Where did our parents live? As we chatted back and forth, Martin casually pulled out a picture roll which he had in his bag. Seeing it lying on the table, one of the men asked what it was.

'It's a picture,' replied Martin, 'but it's a special one – it's full of meaning. Would you like to see it?'

Loud grunts of assent. So Martin spread it open on the table, placing a glass on each corner to hold it flat. The title across the top read *The Two Ways*. It showed a path coming up from the bottom right-hand corner and then dividing into two. One path led steeply upwards on to a beautiful mountain top brilliant with light. Across the entrance to this path stood a deep red cross, so that all who wished to go up had to pass through the low door in the cross. The other path led downwards and ended abruptly on the edge of a precipice. A young man was shown tumbling headlong over the edge into the blackness below. A crowd of people were approaching the road junction — easily recognisable people: a woman carrying her goods to market, a smartly dressed man with his black Muslim *songkok*, a schoolgirl, her head covered with a lacy *selendang* ... they had to choose which way they would go.

Graphically Martin explained the Christian message behind the picture and put the choice there and then to the men in the

123

coffee-shop. Where were they heading for? What choice would they make?

Many thoughtful questions were asked as the men discussed the poster back and forth. One man, Ngerti, seemed particularly interested. He was the village schoolmaster and clearly took the lead. When we finally said we must be getting home, he insisted that we should come back again.

'There are many people here who would listen to what you say. Come back soon and teach us. Just ask for me next time and I'll soon gather a crowd.'

As we cycled home we excitedly discussed plans for returning.

'I think we ought to tell some of the Kabanjahe Christians about this,' Martin said. 'Maybe some of them would come with us.'

But Sitepu was decidedly dubious when we told him about our visit to Lingga. 'It's no use going there. That's the centre of our Karo tradition. No one in Lingga would become a Christian. And yet,' he added relenting, 'on second thoughts you might as well go back again. You need to learn our Karo customs, and Lingga would be the best place for you to pick them up.'

With this not very encouraging response in our ears, we diffidently related our experiences in Lingga to one of the church elders, Damai, a warm-hearted young father of seven children, whose dark eyes twinkled merrily whenever he smiled. To our amazement he was quite enthusiastic, and we were even more surprised when he told us he had been brought up in Lingga.

'Ever since I became a Christian I've wanted to go back to tell them the good news. But I always felt like Sitepu — nobody in Lingga would listen. Yet if Ngerti said they are keen to learn it's worth trying! Why don't we fix a time to go? I can get several others to come along with us. Let's try!'

A week later a group gathered, ready for evangelism in Lingga. 'This is Bapa Bahtera,' Damai said, introducing his plump and smiling friend. ('Father of the Ark,' translated Martin to himself. 'What a glorious name!') 'And this is Bapa

Ravenna,' Damai went on introducing a rather shy, very dark-skinned man. 'He's a Sinulingga, related to the old king of Lingga, you know. He's told one of his junior relations that we'll be meeting in his house. So they are all expecting us. Now, let's pray before we go.'

It was already dark as the team set out on their bicycles, because most villagers work in the fields until sundown and then return home to wash and cook a meal; it would be useless to expect anyone to gather before eight p.m. Martin rode the smart new bicycle I had bought him in Singapore. Its gleaming lamps and flashy dynamo were the objects of much admiration. However, he was soon to find that modern technological advances were not always the answer to problems: the more pot-holed the road became, the slower he had to pedal, and the more dimly his headlight shone. In the worst parts where they had to get off and walk he had no light at all. Our Karo friends, however, who managed with little oil lamps, enjoyed a continuous steady glow!

For several weeks meetings were held upstairs in the home of Bapa Robinson. (Had he named his eldest child after the legendary traveller who was surnamed Crusoe, I wondered?) Bapa Robinson was a 'junior relation' to Sinulingga, who therefore had the right to commandeer his home for the evening. The set-up seemed odd to us, but he accepted it with good grace and made the team welcome. Ngerti, the village school teacher, never missed and was always eager to learn.

Then the team realised they were rather hidden upstairs, so the following week, Bapa Robinson was told that they would like the meeting downstairs in his shop. With two pressure lamps gleaming brightly in the doorway, larger crowds gathered after that. The sacks of fertiliser were pushed up in one corner. Cigarettes, tin mugs and the usual jumble of a village store lined the shelves. But all eyes were on Damai, sitting cross-legged and pointing to a roll of Bible pictures which he had hung from a nail on the wall. So vivid was his description of the rain lashing down on the Ark, that the audience visibly shivered. They could almost see the drowning people, almost hear the crash of thunder as the heavens emptied.

'And who were the ones who were saved?' finished up Damai, his dark eyes flashing a challenge. 'Only those who believed in the one true God, and who did as He had said.'

After two months of weekly meetings, twenty people in Lingga said they would like to prepare for baptism, and were willing to start on the year-long course of instruction.

Writing all their names down was an unexpectedly difficult task. The Dutch church ruling had been that, to register someone for baptismal preparation, his parents' names must be put down too. This ruling carried on after the Dutch left. But Karo custom forbade anyone to say their parents' real names (other than father of so and so, which was how they were commonly called). So to elicit their parents' names from the old grannies, when no one else could remember them, was an amusing process.

'It's the same name as that tree,' they would hedge, unwilling to state it themselves. So the game of guessing began.

'Which tree?'

'The one you pass going down to the river. Past the clump of bamboos.'

'Oh, the sago tree!'

'No, no — Further on — just by where that big stone juts out.'

'Oh, you mean the banyan tree?'

'Yes, yes,' the old granny grinned.

'Write down Banyan Tree,' the elder stated.

'No, no,' granny interrupted; 'that's not right.'

'What's wrong? You said Banyan Tree!'

'Just one word, not two,' mumbled granny.

'You mean, just Banyan?'

'Yes, that's it,' agreed granny smiling, pleased that they were able to write it down without her having actually uttered the word.

To find out the names of all the children was even more difficult. The Karo Church practised infant baptism. The children of unbelievers had been offered to the spirits when they were born. Now the parents were becoming Christians, they wanted the whole family to be baptised together. They wished

126

for a public token that their children were no longer under the spirits' sway.

'Right,' said Damai, indicating one of the new converts. 'You start first and give us the names of all your children.'

'Well, there's Kelung. He's the eldest. Fine lad, too, taller than me already. Then come Meri and Rasmita. No no — Parde comes next. Before Rasmita. At least I think so. Wasn't she born that year the harvest was so dry? Wife! Who's the older, Parde or Rasmita?'

'Wife', sitting in the gloom with the other women at the back, set him right on that point.

'Then there's Selamat — he's the youngest. But let me see, I must have left someone out. How many names have I said?'

Damai solemnly counted them. 'Five,' he announced.

'One short!' exclaimed the puzzled father, scratching his head.

Whispers were heard at the back from where 'wife' was sitting. They were passed forward. Someone whispered into the father's ear. Light slowly dawned all over his face.

'Of course,' he smiled. 'Little Saman! I knew there was another one! Write down Saman,' he ordered, well pleased at his own cleverness at remembering them all.

Later we learned another piece of Karo culture. Each *kampung* is divided into *kesains* (sections) which function quite independently of each other. People often know little of what is going on in another *kesain.* We thought we had entered Lingga, but really we had only entered one *kesain.* So began a new plan. While two of our Karo colleagues held the main meeting in Bapa Robinson's house, the others visited an eight-family house in another part, hoping to gain an entrance there. Soon we were welcomed in two *kesains* for weekly meetings, and numbers grew faster than ever.

This experience in Lingga made us realise that Karoland was wide open to the gospel. Animism no longer had a tight hold on the people. As education increased and their horizons broadened, the people began to see how ridiculous it was to tie down one's god to a river or tree. Who would you tell your son to worship when he went down to Medan to study at a univer-

127

sity? He could not take the familiar gods of his local streams and volcanoes with him. God must surely be greater than that!

Martin and I wondered about starting evangelism in other villages. How should we go about it? Lingga had thrust itself upon us, but nothing else opened up quite so quickly.

'Remember that you're not here for evangelism,' Sitepu remarked to us rather strictly one day. 'You don't know the Karo culture, so leave the non-Christians to us. Your work is in the Church.'

Certainly by that time we had built up a fairly full programme. On May 7th, 1962, — six weeks after we had moved into our new home — Martin wrote home to his mother:

Time flies by in a busy but happy whirl, and again it is time to drop you a line . . .

Perhaps I should give you some idea of our weekly programme, for it is now settling down a bit — although, of course, there are always additions and variations on an original theme!

Most Sundays we shall be out in a 'kampung' or town, speaking at these different churches and trying to get some additional life into them. Yesterday, we were at Brastagi, some eight miles from here, and then when we got back in the evening I preached in the two big wards of the local hospital. Monday morning Elizabeth teaches the Bible in the local Church High School from 7.15–9.30 a.m.; she then has her language teacher 4–5 p.m. I lead the Youth Bible Studies 6–7.15 p.m., then go straight to one of the evening Cottage Bible Studies which are held most evenings in different homes: this lasts until about 10 p.m. On Tuesdays Elizabeth has a Women's Meeting 2–4 p.m. (if we are in Kabanjahe on Sundays she also has a Women's Meeting here in the afternoons). Tuesday evening I go to another Cottage Bible Study. On Wednesday I teach English Bible to the son of the Head of the Church — he is going to Bible School in August to train for the ministry. In the evening it's the Cottage Bible Study again. Wednesday afternoons Elizabeth has a Training

Class for the leading Church women. On Thursday I go to Brastagi for a Training Class for Church leaders 6.30–10 p.m. In the afternoon Elizabeth has a Women's Meeting 2–4 p.m. On Friday she has her language teacher again from 4–5 p.m., and I teach 7.15–10.30 a.m. in School. In the evening I again go to a Cottage Bible Study. On Saturday evening I take a group of local Christians to a heathen 'kampung' called Lingga . . .

We get up about 6.30 a.m. generally, have our times of prayer and Bible study, and then Elizabeth gets breakfast. She makes excellent pancakes, pastries and scones to replace the missing bread! Much of the morning seems to be taken up with sweeeping, cleaning the stove, filling bottles with oil, washing, marketing, etc., and then very often visitors occupy even more time still. Otherwise the mornings are devoted to preparation of talks and language study.

There was plenty to keep us occupied within the Karo church, but the openness we had seen at Lingga, and the hunger for Christian teaching apparent wherever we went, made us long to reach out further. Surely there were other *kampungs* just as ready as Lingga to learn about Jesus Christ! We prayed together often, asking that we should know the best way to reach them. We were well aware of how new we were to the situation and how easy it would be to go about things the wrong way.

The beginning of God's answer to our prayer came that very next week. Damai and Father of the Ark called on us one day and we invited them to sit down. Damai brusquely scattered the group of local children who had immediately gathered on the pavement outside our door to stare. Then turning to Martin he said earnestly, 'Our visits together to Lingga have made us realise that we know so little. How can we teach these animists when our own knowledge is so poor. We want you to hold a class specially for elders and deacons. We want to know our Bible better and our Christian faith better. Please will you teach us?'

Martin looked at me with a sense of inadequacy in his eyes.

We were only new missionaries. It was barely two years since we had left England. And here were the local church leaders asking for deeper teaching. Yet what great things might happen if the elders and deacons were mobilised into working for Christ! Martin looked through his diary, and finding that every evening was booked, suggested they came between six and seven p.m. on Tuesdays. So began a wonderful opportunity. Half a dozen men came the first time and numbers grew to twelve or fifteen. Week by week Martin went through with them the basics of our Christian faith. They hunted through the Bible together to learn more about each person of the Trinity, how great and glorious They are and what They have done for Mankind. They studied the Christian life: how to grow as a Christian, overcome temptation, live by the power of the Spirit. The men were thrilled, and when the time came for a more widespread evangelism of the whole area, they were ready to take over.

As we had mentioned in our letter, each evening a Cottage Bible Study was held in town. Sitepu had divided Kabanjahe up into six areas, and the Christians in each area were invited to meet together on a different night of the week for Bible study and discussion. Martin made the rounds of these groups evening by evening, expounding the passage given and frequently urging the necessity of getting out and telling others about our Christian faith. But there was no apparent response.

One Monday night early in July, Martin was sharing the Cottage Bible Study with one of the Karo Bible Teachers. Father of Gabriel, as he was called, was rather a stiff and greying old man whom we had been inclined to dismiss as old-fashioned. Until we heard his story . . .

During the war of independence against the Dutch, he had been seized one day by Indonesian soldiers.

'You're a traitor!' they shouted. 'You follow the Dutch religion. You must be on their side. We're going to kill you!'

'Drag him down to the river,' yelled another man, shaking him roughly. 'Kill him by the river and offer his blood to the river god!'

'Kill him! Kill him!' the soldiers shouted as they hustled him along.

Father of Gabriel had no time to think, but as they reached the bank he made his voice heard.

'Can I ask just one thing before I die?'

'What is it?' the officer demanded roughly.

'I want to pray.'

The officer hesitated. 'Well, all right, though religion can't help you much now!'

On the green bank of the swiftly flowing river Father of Gabriel knelt down and spoke quietly with his God. He told Him he was ready to die — glad to be coming — and he asked forgiveness for his fellow countrymen, who were about to commit this crime. Then he stood up calmly and faced them all.

'I'm ready,' he said simply.

The officer was astounded. Never before had he seen anything like this. He tried to speak, but the words seemed to stick in his throat. Finally, he stammered out, 'Go! Go into the jungle. Run for your life. And don't let me ever see you again.'

Seventeen years later God was still using his elderly servant.

As the discussion time was about to begin, Father of Gabriel suddenly straightened his stiff old back.

'I've had an idea,' he said.

Everyone looked his way. Father of Gabriel did not often come out with bright ideas.

'We ought to be sharing our good news with others. We ought to be going out into all the *kampungs* round about for evangelism. Now, listen to me, here's my idea. We, the Monday group, will be responsible for the village of Ketaren. The Tuesday group can take on Samura. The Wednesday group Sumbul. Where else should we go?'

Suggestions came flowing in, and so it was decided that each group of Christians would be responsible for one outlying village. As the others met for Bible study on the given night, two members would go out to the village and start evangelism. Thus six villages would be reached every week with regular Christian teaching.

131

Martin came home that evening elated. Once again God had shown His will. He had kept us from making mistakes in organising it all ourselves. And now it was to be on a much wider footing: six villages reached for Christ and that by the Karo Christians themselves!

Opportunities began to snowball. The letter home describing the elders' request for more teaching also went on to say:

My weekly visit to Brastagi looks as if it's going to develop into quite a big thing with leaders from Surbakti and other 'kampung' churches joining the Brastagi elders in study with me. We get such amazing opportunities here, but could do with more workers and more experience. The Sunday School teachers are now coming weekly to have a Preparation Class.

This latter class fell to me, as my Bible College Principal had given such excellent teaching on this subject. With the help of my language teacher I translated all my college notes into Indonesian and the Sunday School teachers found them a tremendous help. In fact, years later we heard that some of them were using these same notes to give lectures on Sunday School teaching all over Karoland.

Within a few weeks of our settling in, Sitepu requested that we start something for the young people in Kabanjahe. He left the running of the meeting in our hands, but stipulated that it must be held in the church.

'I want to stop them being shy of coming into the building,' he explained.

'Pity he won't let us hold it in our own home,' I grumbled to Martin afterwards. 'A dozen youngsters coming every week will be lost in that barrack of a church. Why, it seats a thousand people!'

But Sitepu knew what he was doing, and later, when the numbers had grown, they would never have fitted into our downstairs room, anyway.

It was the beginning of the dry season when we started and

132

the high winds covered everything with a gritty film of dust. The one compensation was the glorious sunsets which swept the sky night after night at dusk. As we walked through the town for our first young people's meeting the sky appeared particularly beautiful. It looked like a gossamer Japanese painting, with the majestic volcano dominating the foreground, and dark green pine-trees silhouetted against the rapidly changing pinks and orange and gold. The steady stream of smoke from the huge crater slowly blended into the exotically-coloured clouds.

A small group of teenagers were standing shyly by the door to greet us. In the gathering dusk, the inside of the large wooden church appeared more gloomy than usual. We hastened to switch on all the lights but found they consisted only of three bulbs hanging one behind the other down the centre of the church.

'It won't be easy to make this bright and attractive,' Martin whispered to me; and then went on in a louder voice in Indonesian, 'Come on everyone! Let's all sit together at the front. We'll start off with some singing. Now, who knows a good one to begin with?'

We bunched up together in the first two long wooden pews, boys sitting strictly on one side and girls on the other. Singing in such a vast building was difficult at the best of times. This evening, as they were shy of us and shy of each other, we could hardly get a peep out of them.

'Isn't there a piano in the church, or an organ?' asked Martin in desperation. 'I know the Sunday services are always unaccompanied but surely there is something.'

There was a long pause and then Rasmita volunteered, 'There is an organ at the back, but it's broken and no one knows how to mend it.'

'I'll have to get Elizabeth to bring her piano accordion next week to liven things up then. We'll leave the singing and I'll show you these pictures.'

It was hard work, week by week. We felt we were not getting through to the young people, and they would not loosen up. Many times I complained to Martin, 'If only we could have

133

them come to our home. It would be so much easier!' But we were under Sitepu's authority and had no choice.

'We must think through a complete new programme for the Youth,' Martin stated one day. 'We're not getting anywhere at all with them. What can we do to liven things up?'

'Well, first of all the singing is appalling,' I commented. 'They won't follow the lead I give them with the accordion, because they've *always* sung their hymns at a snail's pace. They've never heard it done another way.'

'Sometimes in church,' Martin twinkled, 'I sing the tune to myself at the normal speed, and I've finished a whole line before they're on to the third note!'

'I know that! We must teach them some new ones. Songs they've never sung before, so they've never heard them sung slowly. Why don't we translate some? Something with good words and a really catchy tune?'

'That's a good idea. Get some paper and a pencil and we'll work on it right now!'

'How about giving them a bit of church history too?' one of us asked later, when the rough draft of our first song was completed. 'I'm sure they don't know anything of how Christianity spread to all parts of the world.'

'Yes, we could give them an up-to-date picture of the Church throughout south east Asia today,' the other added. 'We could take one country each week. It would help them to be interested in Christians in other places.'

'Good. It could be like an evening Bible class: some Bible study, a bit of church history, current Christianity, and some good singing and quizzes to liven things up.'

'And we ought to get them inviting their friends. Let's set ourselves a target. Perhaps we could get forty teenagers coming. Wouldn't that be wonderful!'

The plans caught on and at last we seemed to get on the wavelength of the young people. They were thrilled at the new horizons which were being opened up to them, proud to be members of this world-wide church. Snatches of the hymns we taught them could be heard in the market-place and on the road to school. Within a few months, our target of forty was reached.

A nucleus began to form of young people who were keen to learn all they could about Christ and to put Him first in their lives.

Village evangelism, training of elders, Sunday-School-teacher training, young people's work — the wide opportunities came crowding in.

Perhaps the work which brought most variety was our Sunday preaching. We were deeply aware that we were only in Karoland as visitors, so Martin made the rule that he would not go anywhere unless he was invited. But requests soon came rolling in for us to visit many of the surrounding *kampungs*. Sunday by Sunday we travelled to different places to spend the day and to preach at the morning service. It meant that within a few months we had a good knowledge of the district.

Surbakti was one of the first *kampungs* where we spent a Sunday. Although it was only five miles away, the roads were so bad it took us over an hour to cycle there. However, the countryside as usual was glorious: bright blue sky with patches of snow-white clouds scudding in front of the wind; luscious green fields, interspersed with clumps of dark pines or small bamboo thickets; and a wide variety of wild flowers tossing their gay colours in the breeze along the edge of the stony road.

Surbakti had been completely burnt to the ground during the scorched-earth policy of the war. It now consisted of row upon row of dreary little wooden houses. Unlike the well-built church of Kabanjahe, this village one had plaited bamboo walls and a bare earth floor. The pews were wooden planks nailed on to short stubs of tree trunks. A hundred or more villagers crowded to the service, so there were few empty seats.

It was monotonous for us to sit through the first part of the service. We could understand little Karo in those early days. The local elder droning on in his parsonical voice gave us ample time to meditate on how far missionaries export their Western culture along with their Christian faith. If I shut my eyes and used a little imagination, I could easily have been in a small church in the West with the vicar exercising his ministerial vocal chords. And yet these were people hungry to learn, as we soon found out. They listened attentively to Martin's

135

preaching in Indonesian and delightedly bought up all the Christian books we had brought with us.

'Thank you for your sermon,' one after the other said as they came to shake hands with us afterwards. They were rough brown hands used to hours of wielding a hoe in the fields, but warm with their welcome for us.

'Everyone is welcome to come to my house after lunch,' the elder called out. 'There'll be a chance to ask your questions and get to know the missionaries better. Tell your friends who weren't in church to come too!'

As the congregation dispersed we were taken to a large house on the outskirts of the *kampung* where the elder's wife and daughter had been busily preparing a meal. The other elders and deacons joined us, and after we had eaten, some forty people crowded into the main room and plied us with questions. How could they get their church really alive and witnessing, they wanted to know. We felt terribly inadequate, but they expressed much appreciation for what was said.

As it grew time to leave we too had a chance to ask some questions. Had there been a church in Surbakti for a long time? How had they managed during the war against the Dutch?

The elder swept his arm in a wide gesture.

'You see this lovely house,' he said, 'so different from all the other ones in the village. We had little warning that day that our enemies were coming — only a few minutes to gather some essential things. I was responsible for the church's precious Bibles and hymn books. They were too heavy to take with us, so we hastily dug a hole under the house and buried them. As we were all running for our lives, I saw flames begin to leap up from the eight-family houses at the far side of the *kampung*. "O, Lord, what shall I do?" I prayed. "If our house burns down the books will all be spoiled. I haven't put them deep enough to withstand the heat from such flames. Please Lord, don't let our house burn!" The amazing thing was that although the flames swept through the *kampung* this house remained unharmed. Months later, when it was safe to come back, I dug up the Bibles and hymn books again, and they were perfectly all right!'

As we cycled home I reflected that the same God who had

been watching over me in north China knew how to keep his children in Sumatra too. They had prayed to Him and found Him to be trustworthy. God had not let them down.

Chapter Eleven

Ups and Downs

IT WAS THREE A.M. and the alarm clock was ringing. 'Are we being fools?' Martin groaned to me as his hand stretched out sleepily to shut off the bell. I was inclined to agree with him, struggling to open my eyes. But it was too late, as we had promised to be ready. A friend's jeep would soon be arriving to take us near the foot of the great volcano Sebayak.

'Come on, you won't feel so bad when you've had some breakfast,' I urged. 'I've got some rice over to make into porridge. It'll only take a few moments.'

My sister, Mary, had come to stay with us for a four-week visit and we had saved up our climbing expedition until now, so that she could come too. Our Karo friends told us, 'If you want to climb a volcano you must start well before dawn. During the day strong winds whirl around the mountains and it is dangerous to be up there.'

With some breakfast inside us, and the fresh breeze from the moving jeep in our faces we soon felt better. The three Karo friends who were acting as our guides were in jovial mood.

'Perfect day for the climb,' commented one, glancing at the sky which was already faintly streaked with grey. 'We'll get to Dolu just as dawn is breaking. That's as far as the jeep can go.'

The picturesque village of Dolu snuggled right at the foot of the huge volcano. The village people had channeled the sulphurous stream which led from the hillside into a network of irrigation canals spreading out over the wide valley. We picked our way along narrow footpaths following the water. I dipped my fingers in and was surprised to find how warm it was in the chill of the morning. Mary sniffed my fingers.

'They smell like bad eggs,' she commented, grimacing.

Everywhere the smell was growing stronger, the clinging sulphurous smell which hung over the valley. It was not only the water: the soil itself, the trees and wayside plants all appeared steeped in it.

'It's exciting,' I remonstrated, sniffing deeply. 'I've never smelt anything like this before. If it's that strong here, whatever will it be like at the top?'

We pressed on, leaving the beautiful valley behind us. The path up the mountainside was indistinct, and frequently branched in several directions. But our guides knew the way well and did not hesitate. The muddy lower parts made walking difficult and we slithered about among the tangle of jungle creepers. There was scree higher up, loose and easily dislodged. The towering trees gradually receded. After two and a half hours of steady climbing one of the men called back, 'There's the edge of the crater!'

We looked up to see the dark jagged edge not far above us. An exhilarating scramble up the last few yards followed, and we gazed into the immense crater beneath us. It was not shaped in a circle, as I had imagined, but lay as a vast sprawling cavity cut out of gaping black rock. Giant boulders littered the floor, and a pale blue pond lay at one end. The sides were streaked with splashes of vivid yellow where the sulphur-heavy smoke gushed out. The noise of the pressure escaping sounded like an old-fashioned steam engine. We had to shout to make ourselves heard.

'What are these cigarettes here for?' I yelled to Martin. His eye followed the direction my finger pointed, and saw two cigarettes stuck in the fork of a stick which had been spiked into the earth.

'They must be gifts to the spirits,' he shouted back. 'Fancy using cigarettes!'

Our Karo friends came and stood beside us as we surveyed the scene. 'Yes, the animists are very afraid of Sebayak,' they shouted through the noise. 'They'd never dare do this, either,' one of them added, picking up a small stone and hurling it into the chasm below. 'They'd be afraid the gods in the volcano would be angry and wake up. We Christians always throw stones when we're up here, just to show we're not afraid.' He threw another one down into the depths. We watched it bounce against the steep sides of the crater until it finally rolled to a stop at the bottom. Standing there side by side, we all joined in, sending our stones hurtling after his. Our action brought with it a curious feeling, something of a mixture of schoolboy daring and adult carefully-meditated action. By it we were all affirming our faith in the one true God.

For some time before we made this expedition Martin had been wondering if he could manage it. Every now and then he had trouble with breathing. It started to show itself soon after we reached Kabanjahe. Some nights he hardly slept at all because of it. I propped him up with pillows and cushions and he would sit through the long hours, breathing heavily and yet never seeming to get enough air into his lungs. Yet he was basically fit and tough, and refused to worry about it.

Towards the end of Mary's stay we took her with us for a few days' holiday. By then we had been in Karoland about six months and felt ready for a break. The beautiful Lake Toba stretched its immense length of eighty miles between the mountains to the south of us. One of our Karo friends owned a lodging-house in the small town of Prapat on the edge of the lake, and he offered us a couple of rooms there for a few days.

The five-hour bus journey to Prapat was hot and tiring, but it gave Mary a good chance to see more of the country, and we were all looking forward to a good rest when we arrived.

Unfortunately for Martin, this was not to be. His breathing-trouble came back far more severely, and as night came on he was gasping for breath. The rooms we had been lent were small and stuffy, with just enough room for a double bed, cupboard and chair. But they opened out on to a long communal terrace overlooking the lake. Here we made Martin as comfortable as we could, on an upright chair. Mary tucked a cushion into his back, and I fetched a blanket as the nights were chilly. With the fresh air now blowing in his face he found he could breathe more easily. The exhausting gasping for breath was eased, but to go to bed in that stuffy room was out of the question.

He sat there all night, watching the lights of an occasional car wind up the headland on the far side of the lake. A silent praying mantis crept out on the terrace wall and performed a slow ghostly dance along the edge. He watched it working its way noiselessly over the stones, its lithe body swinging in a graceful movement. The moon stole out over the lodging-house, rising higher and higher until her shining reflection could be seen in the depths of the lake. Still she sailed on as the hours went by, riding her invisible chariot through the maze of the Milky Way. At long last the bulbuls began to warble, and the brilliance of the moon paled in the light of dawn.

This was to be the pattern for many nights to come.

As neither of us had any medical knowledge it took us some time before we realised that Martin's trouble was asthma. With the onset of day Martin would feel better, and his strong con-stitution made him able to manage on very little sleep. He was always one to make light of illness.

Mary's holiday came to an end. We pressed on with our weekly tasks. Opportunities for a widening ministry grew ever greater. But I was worried. It was now the months preceding Christmas and the rainy season. The cold, wet days lowered Martin's resistance. He was obviously not well, yet we could not lay a finger on the trouble, or on what it was that came over him as evening drew on. We knew his breathing was made worse by the Karos' love of tobacco. But he would cycle slowly off to an evening cottage meeting feeling already tired and constricted in the chest. Two or three hours' discussion in a smoke-filled room put the cap on it. It was all he could do to sit through the meeting and try to make a useful contribution. He avoided his friends offers to walk home with him. He knew he could only go at his own pace.

One evening he could hardly make the half-mile home after the Bible study. It was very slightly uphill, so he found it im-possible to cycle. He staggered along a few yards at a time, leaning heavily on his bike, and then collapsed on the pave-ment. After some time he managed a few more steps and then had to sit down. I had long since gone to bed and was lying awake in the semi-gloom of our tiny oil lamp, wondering why

Martin hadn't arrived home. Had the meeting gone on longer than usual? It sometimes did. Was Martin worse? Should I get dressed and go and meet him? But he could be coming home by several alternative roads and I might easily miss him.

At last I heard the sound of someone downstairs. It was Martin. He had managed to reach the front door and was sitting on the floor just inside, with his head bowed and his shoulders heaving. The bicycle lay outside where he had dropped it, the front wheel still spinning round.

'Darling, are you all right?' I gasped. 'Come, sit in a chair, not on the cold cement floor!'

I dragged a chair to the doorway and helped him into it, brought the bike in, and flung the door wide open so that he could have as much fresh air as possible. He could not manage to climb upstairs, so I made up our camp bed next to the dining-table. After a long rest he managed to crawl into bed.

'You really must see a doctor,' I pleaded when at last he was comfortable. 'There must be something radically wrong.'

'I don't like to trouble him,' Martin countered. 'He always seems so busy. He's the only doctor in the whole area and has much more serious things to cope with than my breathing trouble.'

'Yes, but you're just knocking yourself up,' I remonstrated. 'Suppose you'd never managed to get home and lay there all night on the pavement. You could have caught pneumonia! I'm going to the hospital myself this morning. You'll be in no state to move. The doctor *must* come and see you!'

I had only been to the hospital a few times before to help with ward services, and now crowds of people thronged the entrance as I arrived. A bus drove up, sounding its horn. Visitors to the wards scrambled out, clutching baskets of food and flasks of hot tea for their relations. Patients were helped out by their friends: one with a blood-stained head bandage, another on a pair of home-made crutches. There was such need, such suffering everywhere. How could I push in front of them all? And where would I find the doctor anyway? He had newly arrived in Kabanjahe and I had never met him.

'Keleng!' I caught sight of Damai's brother. We had not realised that he worked in the hospital.

'Good morning, Nyonya,' he greeted me. 'Can I help you?'

I told him that I needed to see the doctor and was immediately shown into a private sitting-room, and brought some tea while I waited.

The doctor could not have been more helpful. To my surprise I discovered that he was a Christian and had been meaning to call on us, only he had been too busy. He came to see Martin that afternoon and ordered various medicines and three days' complete rest.

'Don't hesitate to call me at *any* time,' he said as he left. 'Night or day. I'll come if you need me.'

Such an offer was overwhelming when we knew he was a busy man. And something else which made us gasp with amazed joy was a letter which arrived a few days later from my former landlady in Reading. We had never written to anyone about Martin's illness, but Mrs. Gilkes wrote:

As I prayed for you the other day, I felt something was wrong. I don't know what it is, or which of you two it is, but I feel one of you is ill. I'm asking God to send you a Christian doctor who will be a real help to you.

Seven thousand miles away in Reading! But the God who is real and who was caring for us had prompted her to pray for the very thing we needed. This Christian doctor was God's gift to us in the months when we were learning how to cope with Martin's asthma.

The three days' rest worked wonders. Martin revelled in the unaccustomed luxury of having time to read or lie back and listen to our favourite records. But as soon as he was up again the asthma returned.

Then I, too, was taken ill with a temperature and sore throat. I had had a month-long cold just after Mary left us and seemed to be dogged by germs. Now we were both in bed! Mother of Pesta soon found out and organised everything for us. Dear warm-hearted motherly little person! She asked Rachel to wash up and clean the house for us, while Rasmita took our washing down to the river to do with her own. Lunch was bought for us at a Chinese eating house. So we were well looked after. And when we remonstrated at all they were doing, Mother of Pesta replied, 'Haven't you left your family to come here and teach us? *We* are your new family now. You must let us do it.'

I was soon up and about again, but to save the extra work involved in cooking, I followed Mother of Pesta's example and often bought lunch out. We discovered that the eating-shop was run by a fine Chinese Christian. To buy lunch there was a help to him, and saved me the trouble of cooking. As he lived just three minutes' walk away across the market I brought the piping-hot food back and we ate it in comfort at home. My meagre knowledge of Mandarin was not sufficient to help him with the Sunday service which was held in his upstairs room. Yet we encouraged this small group of Chinese believers all we could, and kept them well supplied with Christian books.

Three months before he was taken ill, Martin had been asked to organise a day's conference on evangelism for all the church leaders of the district. The evangelistic groups going out from Kabanjahe showed encouraging results, and we longed for this type of work to be done in other areas. So we were thrilled when this request came. Now, as the date drew nearer, Martin was weak with asthma and it looked as though we should reluctantly have to cancel the gathering. Right up to the last moment we wondered what to do.

But we were in Sumatra, not by our own choice, but because we were serving a King. If He wished to use us He would give us the ability to do our work. A few days before the conference, in Martin's daily Bible reading, came the verse: 'My strength is made perfect in weakness.' The overwhelming feeling came to him: this is my King's command direct to me. I may be weak, but God's strength will be with me. We must not cancel the meeting.

On December 12th the area Synod gathered for their quarterly meeting. The delegates stayed the night in town. Next morning, at seven a.m. Martin began his instruction classes: ten hours' teaching on evangelism he gave that day, inspiring the church leaders to initiate it in their own areas. Between the classes he retired to bed while I brought him his meals or a cup of coffee. No one guessed what he was battling with. But God kept His promise. His strength was shown through Martin's weakness; and from that day, evangelism began to spread throughout Karoland. God's timing was perfect. The country was ripe for the good news of God's love in Jesus Christ. People began to turn to Christianity in tens, twenties and fifties. And the work which began then has snowballed out of all recognition as I write this ten years later.

But it left Martin exhausted. That night I woke with a start. I was sleeping on a camp bed so that Martin could be more comfortable on our three-foot ten-inch 'double' bed. I could hear the shuddering gasps as he tried in vain to get his breath. Hurriedly I lit the lamp and went over to him. Even in the dim light I could see how pale he looked. I pulled up his pillows again and helped him to a more upright position. The window over our bed did not open, so I could not give him any fresh air. He had taken his usual medicines before retiring to bed but they had not helped. Every breath came in a rasping shudder. The effort of keeping going was exhausting. I was really frightened and looked wildly round for some way of helping him. But there was nothing else I could think of.

'I'll go for the doctor,' I said, mopping the perspiration off his forehead with my hanky. Martin was too weak to protest. 'O God, help him, help him,' I half sobbed as I raced to get my clothes on. 'O God, don't let him die!'

I got my bicycle out and pedalled as hard as I could to the doctor's house on the outskirts of the town. 'Night or day, I'll come if you need me,' he had promised me. Well, this was it. He was up in a flash at my call, hastily gathered a few essentials, and drove on ahead in his jeep. I had left the door unlocked so that he could go straight in. When I arrived back home it was to find the young doctor anxiously watching Martin's blood pressure. In his desire to give some relief he had immediately given an adrenaline and cortisone injection, but without taking time to give the usual initial test dose. He had done this previously with his Indonesian patients without any apparent ill effects, but Martin reacted violently and went into a state of shock.

I believe the Doctor thought he was going to die, and he looked terribly shaken. Helplessly we watched Martin's limp form lying back against the pillows. The doctor kept his hand on Martin's pulse. We both prayed — silently, furiously ... Then the blood pressure picked up, the pulse grew stronger and the doctor heaved a sigh of relief. He stayed until Martin was quite comfortable and had dropped off to sleep. He promised to call again the next day.

We had been expecting a busy Christmas with services held in many churches, but the doctor ordered Martin to have a quiet month with no meetings after dark. It was not what we had planned, and it was frustrating to let slip opportunities where huge crowds could be reached for Jesus Christ. But God could work without us just as well as with us. Our job was to inspire the local Christians and for *them* to do the task.

A stream of visitors came to enquire after Martin's health and to bring gifts of rice or other food. It took hours of my time to sit with them and answer their questions. I tried to shield Martin from seeing all but his closest friends, as he found talking so tiring, but it was touching to see the Karo Christians' love and care. Their generosity and real concern quite overwhelmed us. How heart-warming and yet humbling it was to see their kindness!

Martin was reading the life of Andrew Bonar at this time. Bonar's Christ-like life deeply impressed him and he was much helped by various things Bonar said. Martin quoted him in a letter to a friend: 'We are to be content to labour little ... better do a little with prayer, and in the Spirit!'

He went on to write:

We have been learning about being forced to do comparatively little and now we need to know more about prayer. We are at present stressing prayer very much in our Church work in Kabanjahe, but so often we need to practise what we preach.

147

Just before Christmas I went halfway to Medan for a Christmas celebration for all the women's fellowships throughout Karoland. Our party arrived early so as to get the church ready. There were twenty or thirty women in the large church, arranging flowers and setting the pews ready, when suddenly we heard a cry of pain. Someone had been stung on the cheek by a fierce hornet. As I looked up, screams began to fill the air as others were stung. People panicked and thrashed out at the fiery insects with their long scarves. Then I saw that the hornets were streaming in through a high window at the front near the choir stalls. Evidently they nested in the tall trees just outside and the unaccustomed hubbub had disturbed them. They now started to swarm out on the attack. The only thing to do was to get the window shut before more came in. So I made my way across to it. The hornets were still comparatively few. One could see them flying and duck to avoid them. They appeared to go for those who were flaying around at them the most. But the angry buzzing outside the window grew louder as others searched for the small opening to come in. I managed to close the window without being stung and quite soon we were able to kill all the hornets which had come in. Several women were in awful pain. Some had hornets entangled in their long hair: unlike bees, they can sting again and again. I remembered a friend of ours who had never been able to walk properly again after a hornet attack, and was thankful that nothing worse had happened here.

I thought the meeting would be cancelled for fear of the creatures finding their way in again. But to my surprise everyone carried on as usual. With the church crowded with five or six hundred women and with our lusty Christmas carols enough to irritate any hornets, we kept a wary eye open for signs of the intruders during the whole of the service. A panicky crowd rushing for the doors could cause even more harm now. Fortunately the windows were tightly closed and they did not attack again.

The following day we were both able to attend the first-ever Christmas celebration in the village of Lingga. Our team of church elders had continued steadily with the work there while

Martin had been ill. There were twenty-eight adults attending the one-year's baptismal preparation class. Interest had spread widely through the village and many were ready to listen who before would have been too prejudiced.

Permission was given for us to use the village *los*, the large central meeting-place. With open sides and a corrugated iron roof supported by strong tall pillars, the spacious covered area could easily seat 500 people. Quantities of wide rush mats were spread out on the bare floor. Children crowded into the front and adults behind. Those who were too shy to allow their faces to be seen by the light of the bright pressure lamps stood in the shadows of the houses around. Loudspeakers carried the singing and messages to all parts of the village. What a thrill it was to watch those intent faces enthralled by Damai's graphic telling of the Christmas story, and to know that for many it was the first time they had ever heard it.

Services were also held in several other villages where evangelism had been started.

Our first Christmas Day together dawned clear and peaceful. I had been out in the lanes the day before and gathered armfuls of scarlet poinsettias. Our house looked gay with their bright red petals festooning the walls. The neighbours stared at me. 'What are you doing with those weeds?' they wanted to know.

Standing on our lovely Chinese lacquer trolley was the small Christmas tree we had been given. The fragrance of its furry branches filled the wooden room. Decorations for the tree had been improvised from anything we could find. One box of chocolates, carefully saved up, furnished beautiful glistening ornaments of crimson, blue and gold. A star made from the small circle of foil under the lid of a Nescafé tin gleamed on the topmost twig. Cotton-wool balls gave the tree a snowy effect. The only fly in the ointment came when Rachel, the Bible woman, saw our tree a few days later. 'Cotton wool to decorate a tree!' she exclaimed in horror. 'Why, the hospital can't even get it for dressing wounds. How can you waste it like that!' Needless to say we had no idea how short it was or we would not have squandered it like that.

I gave Martin breakfast in bed as usual — nice and late for us, around seven a.m. He found he was much better if he did not attempt to get up until nearer nine o'clock. There were only the two of us to exchange presents — such a contrast to the large Christmas gatherings I had been used to at home. It taxed all our imagination to find anything to give each other. Martin had bought me a lacy Indonesian scarf such as the women wear over one shoulder. I had asked Mary to buy me a tie clip for him in Singapore, and had carefully stored it away until this day. I had also wrapped up the pocket diary which he had requested from his mother in July. The other parcels from our families did not arrive until late into February and March.

After the 9.30 morning service held in our huge church packed with 1,000 people, streams of visitors came back to our home to bring us the season's greetings. It was such a joy to realise again that we had so many friends. We had been feeling rather depressed at Martin's constant ill-health, feeling we were of little use to the Karo church. But they crowded in — deacons, elders, ordinary church members alike — to show their warm appreciation of our presence.

The Revd. Bukit, next door, had an influx of relations for the festive season. I greeted him over our back wall as I slipped out to prepare vegetables for lunch. 'You must be feeling so *lonely*,' he remarked feelingly. 'How can you celebrate Christmas without any aunts around?'

The afternoon service in the local prison came as a sharp contrast to anything I had done on Christmas Day at home. The water shortage which affected all of us was even more acute there. The prisoners were only allowed to wash once a week. The floors were never cleaned and the toilets stank beyond description. The Karo Christians who came with us made no pretence at hiding their disgust at the conditions. They breathed through their hankies and the women wrapped their scarves across their faces to try to shield their noses from the awful odour. It was almost impossible to get the choir to sing the well-rehearsed pieces I had prepared for them. If it hadn't been such a stink it would have been laughable — all those muffled voices coming from behind the screen of hankies and scarves. But these prisoners were also people whom Christ loved and for whom he was prepared to die. The small group of dirty and dishevelled people moved Martin in a strange way. Graphically he described Christ's love for them and pleaded with them to give their lives to Him. God could make new people out of them.

Soon after Christmas Martin was finally able to wean himself off the asthma drugs. But his resistance must have been low. New Year's Day, 1963, saw him in bed again, this time with a nasty chesty cough and temperature. Our problems were augmented by the fact that the water supply had come to an end. A limited supply came early in the morning to the church office opposite. So each morning at six a.m. I would be out there, waiting to bring home three or four buckets full, before taking Martin his breakfast in bed.

New Year was a most social season in Karoland. Christmas might mean several weeks of lengthy gatherings, organised by every school, church, youth fellowship, etc., but New Year was a time to visit. Calls had to be paid to all the senior relations in one's family and such important people as the mayor, doctor, headmaster and others. For three days I kept the kettle on the boil, and our two dozen glasses for serving tea were utilised to the full. Martin fought his temperature with aspirins and kept the conversation going while I hurried back and forth to the kitchen for more biscuits or hot drinks. I had used some of my precious flour from Penang for a massive baking. We felt sorry for local people who had wanted to make cakes, but our own small supplies would not have gone far if we had shared them around. The economic situation was so bad there was hardly any sugar or flour in the shops. Some Medan friends told us that, in the capital city, people were hardly visiting each other at all, as it only embarrassed the host when he had no sweet-meats to serve.

Then came a lovely surprise. A German missionary lecturing at the Nommensen Theology Seminary at Siantar, some three hours away, heard Martin was unwell. Posts were so unreliable that he would not risk sending us a letter, but he came all the way in person to invite us to spend some days relaxing in his

151

home. He and Martin had shared a room together at a conference more than a year before, and he remembered a small kindness Martin had shown. He begged us to come at once, so we left for Siantar the next day.

This invitation was a God-sent answer to our need. In the friendly atmosphere and comparative luxury of the spacious home, we were both able to relax and recuperate. Wally and Biz were two of the most delightful people we had met. He was big and slow-moving and German, with a kindly warmth which spilled over to everyone. Biz was a friendly, easy-going American with a delightful sense of humour. It was refreshing to be in a cultured home again, with stimulating conversation and broad horizons — just the breath of fresh air we needed.

Our return to Kabanjahe brought added worries. When Martin showed up for his school teaching he found the premises closed. The teachers were on strike for a 100 per cent pay rise. They maintained that it was impossible to live on their present salary. All over the country the white-collar workers were leaving their jobs to work in the fields so that they would at least have food to eat.

Our hearts ached over the state of the country. There was little we could do except to teach against corruption. We knew this was one reason behind the present crisis. The country was riddled with corruption in every walk of life. A lorry-driver came to ask, 'What should I do as a Christian when I'm stopped at some lonely point by a policeman demanding money? They threaten to sue me for dangerous driving if I don't hand it over quietly.'

Another man told us, 'I can't pay my taxes! When I offer the tax officer the correct amount, he refuses to accept it unless I add 20 per cent. And yet he'll take me to court if I don't pay my taxes soon.'

In the privacy of his own home, a teacher shared with us, 'I'm scared stiff. If I fail any one of my class, his relations will threaten to beat me up. I live in this house on the outskirts of the town and it wouldn't be difficult for them to do so.'

The headmaster of our Church Middle School found himself in such a difficult dilemma that he was forced to resign. He feared for his own safety if he continued to stand out against corruption in his school.

Martin was one of the few people from whom no one dared demand a bribe. We were thankful that the Dutch missionaries before the war had been beyond corruption and had established that a foreign *pandita* would never give or receive a bribe. We urged the whole church to make a stand together on this matter because, as a church, we were in a powerful position. Many of the leading citizens were Christians — the mayor, several of the judges, the doctor, and some headmasters. If we stood together as a united body and ruthlessly refused to have anything to do with all forms of corruption, surely we could turn the tide; but the rot was too deep-seated. It permeated society through and through, and no one dared come out openly against it. It was only when President Suharto came to power some years later that the tide began to turn. His government bravely grasped the nettle of corruption and has now largely eradicated it.

But meanwhile we were in need of constant wisdom as to how to behave. Martin wrote home on January 24th:

The English are a bit unpopular in Indonesia these days ... Our suppression of the Brunei revolt and support of Malaysia ('neo-colonialism') is disliked. The government are considering sanctions against us, and English ships and planes may be banned from Indonesia. Then he commented wryly, 'I don't suppose this has hit the headlines in your English papers!'

As Martin's asthma continued to trouble him, we wrote to our Mission doctor in Singapore to ask advice. In reply to our letter we were urged to track down the cause. The doctor said Martin was probably allergic to something. If only we could discover what it was and avoid any contact with it, the asthma should not trouble him any more. We spent futile hours trying first one thing then another. At one time we thought it was the woollen blankets and so I substituted cotton bed-spreads. He slept with a variety of different objects near his pillow to see if they made any difference. The only thing that did seem to help was to sleep downstairs. It made it very awkward, but we put the camp-bed between the wall and the dining-room table and I made a large screen so that it was not obvious to visitors. For months he slept downstairs, occasionally trying it out again upstairs with me, but this usually meant disaster.

One great improvement made at this time was through the kindness of a neighbour who gave us twenty-five watts of his electricity. The town's supply was so poor that private houses could only buy a maximum of 200 watts. This amount was so dearly prized that there was a queue several years long waiting for it! A small device was fitted on to the outside of the owner's front door; if he used more than the 200 watts at one time his supply would automatically shut itself off. It puzzled me why this was always placed outside. It would be simplicity itself for any passerby to plunge the house into darkness, and in the confusion make off with some valuable goods.

Anyway, here we were, the proud possessors of twenty-five watts. Triumphantly we went down the street to purchase a light bulb. It was a little confusing to learn that the lower the denomination of wattage the higher the price. 'Don't you see,' remonstrated the shop-keeper, 'that more people want the lower watts, so we put up the price!' I vaguely remembered my university economics lecturer expounding on the laws of supply and demand, and coming to the opposite conclusion. However, it was no use arguing, and we were only too eager actually to own a light bulb to do so!

Yards of flex were also purchased and we hurried home. We trailed the flex from our neighbour's back yard into ours. One end was plugged into his electricity supply and to the other we attached our bulb. Now as night fell we need not fear the gloom. Wherever we went our bulb came too, like Mary's little lamb. Upstairs or down, we carried it with us, attaching it to a hook in the ceiling. It did not pay to quarrel: the other one could seize the lamp and banish you to utter darkness!

Chapter Twelve

Changes

'DOWN WITH THE British!' 'Ganyang Malaysia!' 'Abolish Britain!' The large chalk letters screamed at us from public hoardings and empty walls. The swift change in public feeling during our brief holiday in Penang was alarming. We British were now apparently even more unpopular in Indonesia than the Dutch. How would it affect our work, we wondered? And it was not a pleasant welcome for Michael Dunn, ex-Merchant Navy officer, who had joined us on the flight back as our junior missionary.

With the formation of the new State of Malaysia on August 31st, 1963, public feeling in Indonesia began to express itself violently. Many took the opportunity to take the law into their own hands. Riots broke out in several places. Highway robbery on the winding road between Kabanjahe and Medan made people frightened to venture far. Two men were reported to have been killed in an ambush. The roads suddenly swarmed with soldiers and we were reminded that we were under a military regime.

To make matters worse, the Revd. Sitepu refused to sign the necessary papers for our visa renewal until the next meeting of the 'Moderamen' (the Central Church Committee). This was to take place only five days before the visa expired. We realised we might suddenly find ourselves thrown out of the country, as our application had not had time to be seen. Apart from everything else, we hated to leave Michael on his own in a strange country, and our first baby was on the way. I was now seven months pregnant, and did not wish to travel more than necessary.

Michael, Martin and I met every day for prayer together.

Systematically we prayed through all the various countries where O.M.F. works, and of course, our own critical situation. Again we told God that we were in Sumatra by His choice, not ours. If He wished us to stay, if He had more work for us to do, we knew He had the power to keep us there. If He wanted us somewhere else we were willing for that too. We believed in a God who was real and could be trusted. In our present crisis we expected to see His hand clearly visible.

Sitepu's fear of committing his church to English missionaries at that time was understandable. What was heart-warming was the Moderamen's response to the situation. They were vehement and adamant that they wanted us to stay. Several told us in private afterwards, 'If you're afraid of anything just let me know.' 'Don't worry while you're in Karoland. You have many friends here. No one will hurt you.'

Armed with Sitepu's precious signature, Martin immediately left for Medan, not knowing that that was to be the day of the worst anti-British rioting. He saw four large demonstrations and almost ran right into one of them. Turning a corner, he saw a mob surging down the street towards him. Fortunately, he was able to take shelter in an office close by, and, feeling rather shaken, watched the yelling crowd jostle past the window. With a start he heard the man behind the counter comment to him in beautiful English, 'Crazy bunch of mixed-up kids!' Martin smiled with relief that there was someone on his side! But the 'bunch of mixed-up kids' made their way to the British Consulate and ransacked the building. The library was burnt down, the garden ruined, and the ground-floor looted. The Consul himself only held the crowd back from attacking him, his wife and child, by standing with pistol at the ready at the top of the stairs and declaring he would shoot the first person who tried to mount. Within a few days, letters were sent to all British subjects in North Sumatra ordering us to be ready to leave at a moment's notice. We must have a bag packed with overnight things and always keep it by us. Yet God kept our hearts at peace. The *Daily Light* reading for September 30th had this verse, 'The foundation of God standeth sure having this seal, The Lord knoweth them that are

His.' And farther on it read, 'I will instruct thee and teach thee in the way which thou shalt go: I will guide thee with mine eye.' We felt sure that the Lord knew us; He knew our situation and all about us, and He would show us what to do. In the meantime we had no indication from Him that we should consider leaving, so went quietly on with our work.

On October 4th Martin wrote home:

Last week we had news from one of the 'kampungs' that God has begun to work in an unusual way there. Many of this formerly very anti-Christian 'kampung' now want to join the church in faith in Christ. They have large numbers asking about the Christian faith. Children, too, are crowding into their Sunday School, and it seems God wants to save many. But the Christians there are quite recent believers and they felt inadequate to deal with this situation. They therefore came to us for advice, and I felt it right to give them two days and a night in their kampung to teach, answer questions, etc. (They agreed to stop all work in the fields for these two days.) It was certainly a more than worthwhile time — but exhausting! I left here after breakfast on Tuesday and was hard at it until leaving there again the next day about 2 p.m. We worked until midnight and then I stupidly got asthma and had a poor night. But the night was too short for me to be able to take a pill, lest it left me too drugged next morning! The next day began at 5.30 a.m. God is really at work in unusual ways here these days and it is a thrill to be part of His work . . . Life is full but very good indeed!

This *kampung* Martin visited was called Seberaya. From the start of missionary work it had been adamantly anti-Christian because of the strange legend of the Green Princess. The path leading into the village drops down into a sudden deep fault, and a cave in the hillside there was pointed out to Martin. The local legend told of a village girl who had got herself into trouble and was discovered to be pregnant. Banished from the village by her family and friends, she found refuge in this cave.

157

No man in the village would confess to being the one implicated, and the injustice of the sentence was demonstrated when the girl finally gave birth. Triplets were born to her; and most extraordinary they were. One was a huge snake, one an iron cannon, and the last a beautiful green princess. The mother died in child-birth but for many years the snake, the cannon and the Green Princess lived together in the cave. At the time of the full moon the snake would venture out and slither through the fields in search of food. His huge tracks could be seen the next morning, and whoever's fields he had been through would be certain of a rich crop. Many villagers assured us that they had seen the scaly snake-tracks with their own eyes.

At last the little Green Princess grew tall and lovely and wished to marry. Suitors came from all over Sumatra, as the fame of her beauty spread far and wide. But the bridal price was found by all to be too high. Her brother the snake demanded a full-grown bullock to be given to him every day. No one was able to meet these expensive demands.

One day the Prince of distant Aceh sailed his fleet to a sandy beach near Medan and marched up into the hills in search of the Green Princess. When the moon was full and her snake brother out hunting, the Prince stole her away and took her back to his ship. But the snake soon discovered the evil plot and hastened through the jungle after them. As he swam through the sea, chasing the fleet, his great tail lashed so furiously that it created a violent storm. The Prince still hoped he would make it until, with a mighty bang, the cannon on the distant hills of Karoland fired at the ship. The force of the shot burst the cannon, and pieces of its iron casing can be found in widely separated areas of Karoland today. The Prince's ship was hit and sank rapidly. Triumphantly the snake rescued his sister and bore her home to their cave again. There she lived to the end of her days — a virgin to the last. And to this day the villagers of Seberaya treasure the relic which she left them: one long hair of her head, wound around on itself to form a large ball. When the first Christian missionary reached Seberaya he was shown this dark ball, which was kept safely in the rafters of the headman's eight-family house. He laughed at the story, but could find no explanation for the ball. It certainly appeared to be human hair, but longer than any hair he had ever seen. They unwound it for more than a mile and still could find no break. Baffled, he could give no other explanation for it. The *kampung* people were triumphant. 'That proves our story is true,' they said. And for nearly fifty years hardly anyone in Seberaya became a Christian. Now at last the break-through had come and some dared to believe in Jesus Christ. Yet their stand was strongly opposed by the followers of the Green Princess.

Our work continued as busy as ever and gradually the political situation cooled down. What hit us most about diplomatic relations being broken off with Malaysia was that all trade with that country had ceased too. We could therefore no longer order any tinned goods from Penang to supplement the local foods. How we marvelled at God's timing for our holiday! We had been able to bring back with us a good store of tinned food. If the holiday had been planned for two or three weeks later we should never have made it.

After a few weeks, Michael Dunn, who had been sleeping on our camp-bed behind the curtains of our guest-room, moved into a room of his own in a Karo home. Here he would have room for all his things and could get to know Karo life for himself at first hand.

In Lingga, where evangelism was first started, the Christians continued hungry for more teaching. As the Saturday evangelistic team was now concentrating on a second group who were preparing for baptism, those already baptised asked for another meeting for themselves. Martin started studying Mark's gospel with them and they were thrilled to learn all sorts of new things which had not come into their preparation classes.

At the first meeting, Pak Robinson (in whose house they used to meet) asked to buy a New Testament.

'Is it for a friend?' enquired Martin, hunting through his bag to find one.

'Oh no, it's for me. Mine's worn out.' declared Pak Robinson, and pulled the tattered book out of his pocket. 'I carry it every-where. If I knock off for a rest in the fields, I read it. Or in the coffee-shop, often someone asks me a question, so out it comes again. It gets passed around for everyone to read it for themselves. It's just worn out. I need to buy another.'

We were encouraged. Pak Robinson was one of many who were beginning to develop a new desire for personal Bible reading.

Three other villages where evangelistic teams were working showed signs of encouragement. Sumbul, where the work took months to get moving, now had a small group of believers. Samura planned their first baptisms shortly, and Ketaren, which had been a hard spot for some time, began to show a breakthrough.

A school teacher remarked to me after class one day: 'All Samura and Ketaren Sunday School children bring tracts and Christian picture-books to school. Other children read them, and even the teachers borrow them and take them home. You will find Christian literature in nearly every house.'

As the months of my pregnancy drew to an end, we again saw God's loving concern for every detail of our lives. Standards in our local hospital were so poor that I felt unhappy to have the baby there. Besides, our kind Christian doctor had left and the next doctor was new and very busy. But God had it all planned for us.

From time to time an occasional foreigner would drive up to our door while holidaying and exploring these 'remote parts'. One such couple had insisted on taking us out to a very smart meal in Brastagi in the only hotel there which kept some remnants of its former glory. As we sat down to the beautifully laid table with its crisp white cloth, they were surprised to see the waiters greeting us like long-lost friends. To them they were just waiters; but to us one was a church elder, another a valued member of an evangelistic team — and all were our friends!

One day a jeep pulled up by our pavement and out stepped a big friendly American. He turned out to be head of all the Goodyear rubber estates in North Sumatra, and a keen Christian. He invited us to visit his estate near Siantar at any time.

'We've a good hospital there,' he added, 'fully equipped with all the latest things from America. If you ever need it, don't forget.' His words remained with us, and when I became pregnant we knew why God had sent him. On one of our visits to Siantar, Biz drove us over to visit him and he gave permission for me to come in for the baby's birth. It was such a comfort to know I could go to a well-equipped hospital like that with a western doctor.

Biz insisted that I come down early and stay with them before the expected date. 'You could never risk the three-hour bus journey down to us. The buses are uncertain and the road so pot-holed you'd probably have the baby on the way!' What luxury it was to move down to her lovely home and have a week's rest with no cares or worries before the great day! Well, I did employ part of the time usefully by sitting my next language examination. The previous one had been taken amongst the hectic preparations for our wedding. Somehow I always seemed to time my language examinations simultaneously with some great occasion.

And a great occasion it was. On Sunday, October 27th, our precious Andrew was born. His lusty cries rang out just as the first hymn began in the Batak church opposite. The two Indonesian midwives were most loving and competent. They gave him a good start in those early days.

But all was not to go as smoothly as we had hoped. Ten days later I came out of hospital to stay a short while with dear thoughtful Biz and her husband before returning to Kabanjahe. Martin had already gone home, when Andrew developed what I thought was diarrhoea. (Looking back now I wonder if it was not the usual loose stools which every new-born baby has.) We took him back to hospital and the doctor prescribed opium drops for him. I thought it sounded a bit peculiar, but I was not medically trained and had every confidence in the doctor.

I tried to give baby Andrew the prescribed five drops that evening but he hated it so much I only got two into him. Next morning he was so sleepy I decided to leave out the medicine with his early feed, but gave him a full dose just before midday. He appeared to be very dopey and after lunch I could not settle for my usual siesta. I sensed something was wrong. The room was cool and shaded, so I did not notice any change in colour, but soon after three o'clock baby Andrew began to look really peculiar. Suddenly his arms went stiffly above his head, his little legs straightened out, and he screamed and screamed. Then he dropped back limply as if he had gone off to sleep. I picked him up and rushed to Wally, who was in his study, and asked if we could phone the doctor. By God's mercy he suggested instead that we should go to the hospital at once, as it often took half-an-hour to get a phone call through. Just as we were getting into the jeep another thought struck him.

'There's a children's specialist here in Siantar. It would only take us five minutes to reach him and twenty-five to get to the hospital. Shall we go there instead?'

Oh, the heart-rending pain of having to make a snap decision on the spur of the moment! I hesitated in an agony. Baby Andrew went into another screaming spasm and then looked as lifeless as before. What should I say? Then it was as if God told me clearly what to say. 'No, let's go back to where he was born. The doctor there knows the drugs he's on. I think that's best.'

We sped along the bumpy road. 'Don't worry about the ruts,' I gasped. 'Andrew won't mind the bounces. Just go as quickly as possible.' Little seven-pound Andrew lay limply in my arms. He had stopped screaming now and his face was as white as a sheet. It looked as though it were carved out of wax — every feature, the curving nostril, the tiny lips, the softly feathered long eyelashes.

It was touch and go. When it was all over I asked how close it had been. The doctor replied, 'The little chap was already knocking on the pearly gates. Fifteen minutes later and it might have been too late.' The amazing thing was that the only way Andrew's life could be saved was by giving him oxygen, and this hospital was the only one in North Sumatra which possessed oxygen cylinders. If we had stopped to phone, or gone to see the children's specialist in Siantar, it would have been too late.

Baby Andrew was eight hours in the oxygen tent. The Matron herself controlled the inflow of oxygen for the first hour or so, and I sat beside them praying she would know the right amount to give. Yet, after the initial terror at Andrew's first few stiffening screams, my heart had been kept by an invisible power. The peace of God truly does pass all human understanding.

Our Karo friends gave Andrew and me such a loving welcome when we arrived home in Kabanjahe. Bags of rice poured in; bananas, vegetables and fruit of all kinds were lavished on us. Shaking hands after a *kampung* service that Sunday, Martin was startled to find a live white chicken thrust into his hands. 'Congratulations on your baby!' smiled the old granny through her toothless gums. It must have been obvious to them all that Martin had never handled a chicken before, as he tried to hold the squawking bird away from his best suit. But others wanted to shake his left hand too, so clutching at the hen and his Bible with his left hand, he continued to receive their warm congratulations! How green I was became apparent when he brought the present home and I had to enlist Rachel's help to deal with the fowl. But it was all done in good humour — they loved being able to show us how to do things. We felt a 'togetherness' when we could share like this.

Michael, who had been living in our home while we were away, had more than his share of troubles. The October–November rainy season was back again and the ground grew sodden with water. Some of it leaked into the deep toilet shaft, making it fill up badly. The stench rose in step with the rising level of liquid until it became unbearable. It was difficult to find anyone who was willing to come to Michael's assistance, but at last after a horrible battle with long bamboo poles the worst of the filth was shifted. The whole town was also suffering from a severe water shortage, which often mysteriously coincided with the rainy season. For ten days they had no water at all and had to exist on what small supplies had been laid in.

By the time baby Andrew and I arrived home the toilet was in working order again, and Martin and Michael had worked hard to fill up the water butts with rain water. It was good to be home, although I was very apprehensive about caring for

Andrew. I had never even held a baby in my arms before, and knew nothing about looking after one except what I had gleaned from the Indonesian midwives. Dr. Spock's book *Baby and Child Care* was promoted to a place beneath my Bible on the bedside table, and became my sole guide.

As I had developed a nasty boil on my finger after Andrew's crisis, we stopped off on the way home to get some medicine for it. 'A combination of penicillin and a sulphur drug should be just the thing,' the doctor assured me. Glad at the prospect of relief from the pain I readily paid the bill.

On my first day at home Martin and Michael had to go to Tigabinanga and I was left on my own. Having fed the baby and washed all the nappies, I sat down with a cup of coffee when I became aware of a strange tingling feeling. I glanced down at my hands. They were covered with red blotches. Quickly I rolled back the sleeves of my blouse. The blotches appeared to be spreading up my arms! What could it be? Was I allergic to something? Had I touched anything strange? The only thing I could think of was the new shawl in which I had wrapped Andrew. Andrew! Whatever it was, it mustn't spread to him! I hurried to find the shawl and wash it thoroughly, hoping that would deal with it. When I had hung it up I was shaking all over and itching violently. I was horrified to find the red blotches were spreading all over my body now. What could it be? I felt tired from broken nights and the delayed shock at nearly losing Andrew. Martin and Michael were miles away; I was all alone and frightened. I sat down in a chair and sobbed. After a long time through the sobbing a prayer managed to steal out. 'O God, show me what to do.'

I think I must have slept. It was midday and Andrew would soon be wanting a feed. The itching was not quite so bad and the red marks appeared not to be spreading any further.

'I won't do anything until the men get back,' I thought. 'Michael's had some medical training. Maybe he will know what it is. And it is no good going to the hospital as this is the day the doctor goes to the leprosarium.'

I didn't want to touch Andrew in case the blotches were infectious. What awful tropical disease might I be giving him?

But his hungry cries made it impossible for me to leave him. I just had to pray and trust. Maybe I should have realised it was only a reaction to the penicillin. Oh, the relief to find this out from the doctor the next day! It was God's mercy too that I had not taken any more of it, or that might have been the end of me.

Meanwhile, Martin and Michael had eventually made it to Tigabinanga, the centre of one of the four 'dioceses' of the Karo church. For months we had been praying for an entrance into this area. We did not know that the man in charge of Tigabinanga Church had heard Martin speak during his first few weeks in Indonesia. 'I can't possibly ask someone who speaks such appalling Indonesian to my church,' was his reaction. So we were never invited. Two years had now passed and, meeting Martin at the central synod, he discovered to his surprise that he could understand every word Martin said. So at last the invitation was given.

Martin ran a short course for the Tigabinanga church leaders in the afternoon and the plan was that after supper they should all go to a *kampung* for evangelism. They had hoped to go in one of the member's cars, but the rainy season made the road hopelessly impassable. Even the main road to Medan had been cut by landslides the previous week. Returning home, Martin had had to walk a forty-minute detour and then pick up another bus on the far side of the rubble. Now, not even cycling was possible. So the party of some ten men waded through the mud for an hour in the gathering darkness. They slithered and slid, with the mud ankle deep in places, while the rain poured through the few antique paper umbrellas. But they had a good meeting and it was thrilling to see how the church leaders were quite happy to walk through the mud and rain for the sake of Jesus Christ.

The walk back to Tigabinanga at midnight was even worse in the pitch dark. However, friendships had been forged, and it was agreed that Martin should return every fortnight for special training-classes for the leaders.

Unfortunately, with the rainy season Martin's asthma grew worse. It had shown tremendous improvement after our holiday, but now he had to resort to sleeping downstairs again and was always on pills. Yet experience had taught us which pills were the best for different occasions, and most of the time he could keep the asthma under control.

Confrontation with Malaysia brought a sea of trouble for the Karo people. They had lost their main buyer for the lush fruit and vegetables which the fertile area produced. Whole fields of cabbages were left to rot where they grew. Lorry drivers suddenly found they had no work. A new price spiral shot up, making shop goods prohibitive. Many people found themselves without a source of income, and nearly everyone suffered in some way.

Again we marvelled at the way God looked after us. During our visit to Siantar we had found some reasonably priced tinned meat, dried milk and jam. We stocked up on this and a mere two weeks later the prices in the same shops had doubled. I was breast-feeding Andrew and felt the need of more milk for myself. When our supplies were nearly ended, we heard that the Karo church had been given supplies of skimmed milk powder from the U.S.A. but no one knew how to use it. So we gratefully accepted some and taught the people how to mix it in with their food. This tided us over for several months: in fact we never completely ran out.

Another answer to prayer strengthened our faith in the God we were serving. At the beginning of the year we had asked God that Martin should be allowed to preach in the great church in Kabanjahe. Sitepu was very particular that all the sermons here should be in the Karo language, although he did not mind the *kampung* people listening to our Indonesian. We felt we could not attempt to learn two languages at once, and so had concentrated on Indonesian, though with Martin's gift for languages he picked up a good deal of Karo on the side.

On December 10th Martin wrote home:

There has suddenly been a change of leaders and as a result I was preaching in the Church here last Sunday! God answers prayer! I prayed and read all the liturgy in Karo — including the Scripture reading — but preached in

166

Indonesian, and then gave a short resumé in Karo. So we hope that everyone will have benefited from it. The Lord certainly helped with the Karo and the sermon seemed to have His power too!

Our work programme continued to be as heavy as ever. This same letter described some of it.

This afternoon I have a meeting of the P.C.C. here and then a meeting for Bible Study this evening as well as school teaching this morning. Tomorrow, is the big three-monthly meeting of the Diocese, so I shall be at that most of the day. Thursday morning I teach solidly all morning, but then am free until Friday evening when I have another Bible Study. Saturday starts the full Christmas programme when I shall be in Medan for the huge Youth Christmas Celebration for the young people from all over Karoland. I shall not get home again until about 3 a.m. on Sunday. On Sunday I preach at the large inter-church open-air witness here. Monday is Lingga's Christmas celebration; Wednesday is the *kampung* of Sumbul; Thursday morning is the large women's Christmas gathering for all the women all over Karoland, and then I come home in time for the school's celebration in the evening. Friday and Saturday both have school's services. Sunday 22nd I hope to go to Tigabinanga for their Youth/Schools Christmas 'do'. Monday I go to the large Leprosarium near here; but in the afternoon beforehand I have the service for the Military and Police. Tuesday 24th is the main Christmas Celebration here in Kabanjahe when I preach again. Christmas Day I hope to be in the 'kampungs' again, while on the 26th and 27th I have smaller services here in Kabanjahe. When one realises that all these services take some three hours each, except the really big ones which can take five hours, one realises that such a programme is quite full. Preparation of messages and sermons must also be fitted in.

It remains a hazy memory now of riding crowded on the

back of a vegetable lorry, through fearful mud and with spinning wheels, to the little village of Samura, at being drenched by heavy rain at the outset of a large open-air service with over one thousand people hastily crushing into the shelter of Kabanjahe's large church; of preaching to the packed church at Munte (Rasmita's home town) where the wide-open doors at the back spread a vista of rice-fields and palm-trees stretching to the foot of the giant volcano — telling the marvel of God become man to a group of six hundred secondary school children, most of whom were from Muslim or Animistic homes; of sharing the glory of God's wonderful love in a picturesque dark wooden church packed with patients suffering from leprosy, their scarred unsightly faces alight with joy at the fact that someone loved them; and of marching on a glorious starlit night with flaming torches, while more and more Christians from all over the town of Brastagi joined us, until the town was ablaze with three thousand lights and alive with the sound of Christmas carols.

Chapter Thirteen

Expansion – and Frustrations

AFTER THE CHRISTMAS and New Year lull we were back into our busy programme again, though this time we took care not to take on quite so much. With the teachers' strike settled, there was a couple of weeks' teaching before the schools broke up again for the Muslim fast-month. It was no wonder the children's education did not progress very quickly, as they seemed always to be on holiday. However, when the schools were in progress we had a marvellous opportunity. I taught in the church high school and Martin in the big government one. Each Friday morning he would cycle there by seven-fifteen a.m. and take a class of ninety teenagers for an eighty-minute period. Extra chairs were packed into the class-room to seat everyone. After a short break he would teach another eighty-minute period, and as the Muslims and Roman Catholics were free at this time they crowded listening around the open windows. It became more like an open-air meeting. Martin's message gripped them, and many of these youngsters started coming to our Monday night Youth Fellowship.

Attendance at the Youth Fellowship had remained a steady forty for some time. Now Martin put it to them. If they had found God to be real, and that becoming a Christian had made a radical change in their own lives, they must share this with their friends.

'Next week,' he urged, 'I expect every one of you to bring a friend. There are crowds of teenagers in Kabanjahe. What a difference it would make if each one was in touch with God Himself!'

'Next week' came and the youngsters rose to the challenge. They brought their friends with them, and the front pews of our vast church began to look comfortably filled, as around sixty-five teenagers sat down. Just as we were about to start the lights failed. An electricity cut had struck that part of the town. The evening was rapidly growing darker and soon it would be pitch black inside.

'Everyone, come along to our house!' Martin announced brightly. 'If we have a cut too, at least our paraffin lamps are working.'

We had been longing to have them all come to our home, although this was not quite as we had imagined it. Our few chairs were quickly removed out to the back, the dining-table shoved against the wall. Rachel and Rasmita appeared with hastily borrowed rush mats for the floor and all sixty-five of us crowded in. There was barely room for everyone, but the jostling and squeezing up engendered a good deal of laughter. The singing sounded great with so many lusty voices in a small area and the varied programme captivated their interest.

Here was the break-through at last! That week marked a turning-point. Numbers steadily climbed up, until week after week we were around the one hundred mark. But what encouraged us most was the changed lives of some of those young people that became the talk of the town. A deputation of school teachers arrived at our front door one day. 'Tell us what you are teaching our pupils,' they requested. 'They are so different now, we hardly recognise them. The lazy ones are hard-working. The cheats and liars have changed.' What an opportunity this was to talk about the power of Christ! The indisputable proof of a radically changed life cannot lightly be ignored.

Masta was one of the teenagers whom we came to know well. His relations lived in Lingga, so he asked to be allowed to join the weekly evangelistic team there.

One evening, lurching along in Father of Pesta's jeep on the way to Lingga, Martin asked Masta about himself.

'I've been a different person since coming to the Youth Fellowship,' Masta commented with eyes shining. 'You see,' he went on, dropping his voice, 'my father sent me to Medan to study at the university. It was all so different after village life — shops glittering with wonderful things, exciting movies,

170

bright lights and lots of friends. It was so hot during the day I hated to study. We'd sleep or lie around and then when evening grew cool our gang would go out on a spree.'

Masta hesitated, looking around to see if anyone else was listening. But the other men were chatting together in the front and the rattle of the jeep made it difficult for anyone to over-hear. He leaned closer to Martin and continued, 'My best friend was killed in a gang fight. It was ghastly. They all came out suddenly against us. They knew we'd been planning to see that film. Their knives were out before we had a chance. It was horrible. Then I saw that he had been badly wounded. I dragged him away. We hid down a dark alley until they'd all gone. But as I watched his face I knew it was too late . . . He died in hospital.'

Masta's face dropped into his hands. His whole body seemed to groan. Martin put a hand on his shoulder but said nothing. The lurch of the jeep threw them closer together. The other men, oblivious, went on chattering in front. At last Masta raised his head. 'When my father heard about it he ordered me home. But I was finished already. I didn't want to study. I didn't feel like eating or doing anything. I was dazed. Life was useless. What was the point of living? Of course Father was furious, but I was too numb to feel his blows or hear his stormy words. I worked at home in the fields for a time, still dazed, still wondering what was the point of going on. Then Father got me this job in Kabanjahe and one of my friends took me along to your meeting. I didn't want to go at first, but it was something to do. And there for the first time I saw people who had real joy. It was fantastic. It bowled me over. And now Jesus Christ has done the same for me,' he added simply. 'Life's worth living again. I've got something to share.'

Some days after that conversation Masta had a shock. Riding down the street towards him on his bicycle was Namaken, the leader of the rival gang in Medan. When Namaken saw Masta, fear sprang to his eyes. He whirled his bike around intending to flee.

'Don't go!' shouted Masta. 'I'm a Christian now. I don't hate you any more. Please don't go!'

Namaken was so taken aback that he stared at his old enemy. With hand outstretched Masta crossed the road to greet him. He told him all that had happened. 'Come with me to our young people's meetings,' he urged. 'Jesus can do the same for you.'

That was how Namaken too found that God was real.

One day a small, thin woman appeared shyly at our door. Although we urged her at once to come in she was very timid and took a great deal of persuading. Her dark pointed head-dress shaded her weather-tanned wrinkled face. Her faded purple sarong hid a figure bent from years of working in the fields. She slipped off her worn leather sandals by the door and perched herself on the very edge of the nearest chair. I hurried to make glasses of hot sweet tea for us all to drink together, and gradually she lost her shyness. She told us she was Adil's mother, and we brightened at the name. Adil was a sixteen-year-old who came to our meetings, but we remembered him best for his pet orang-outang. We had seen the two of them one day romping together. The great monkey had leapt into a young sapling which swayed violently from side to side under his weight. He had then used it as a catapult to shoot him through the air on to Adil's back. And the two of them rolled over and over, laughing, on the grass.

'It's about Adil that I come,' said his mother hesitantly. And then she looked at me with my white skin and smooth hands. 'A Karo woman's life is hard,' she said. 'We work from dawn to dusk and long after. Cooking, cleaning, hoeing, chopping firewood — there's no end to it all . . . But I don't mind working for Adil now that he's become a Christian. He's a different boy. It's a joy to work for him.' Tears were shining in her eyes as she ended and I could feel mine pricking too. What wealth of love and pain and hard work lay under the surface of those words! What joy that a lad becoming a Christian could make such a difference to his mother's life!

We asked the young people if some of them would like to help us with ward services in the local hospital. It gave excellent opportunities for training them in leading a Christian meeting. The braver ones helped at once by announcing the

hymn or reading a passage of Scripture. Soon some over-
came their shyness sufficiently to pray in public. All helped
in singing and chatting with the patients afterwards. It was
a triumphant moment when one of them gave a short talk for
the first time.

The hospital provided fertile ground for the gospel. Patients
travelled in from far and wide. Lying in bed with nothing to do
but think and talk, they were very open to what we had to say.
Once a patient called out to Martin, 'Do you remember me?
I'm from Dolu. You know, at the foot of Sebayak volcano.'
Martin went across to shake his hand and he went on. 'You
came into my coffee-shop that day after you'd been up the
mountain and I've never forgotten. I'm here because I got hurt
in a fight. And I said to myself, "If I was like that white
missionary who came to my coffee-shop, I wouldn't get mixed
up in fights like this" . . . Tell me. What is it about you that
makes you different?'

As Martin talked with him he was ready there and then to
become a Christian.

Another week as Martin visited the T.B. ward one of the
men called out, 'Come up this end. We're all Christians now!'
Sure enough, that group of eight or so up at one end of the ward
had been discussing together all they had heard about God, and
they made a joint decision to become Christians.

God worked in such a wonderful way in that hospital that
nearly every time Martin spent an hour or so visiting there
someone found Christ as their own Saviour.

The power of God was being seen in widening circles
through Karoland. It was not through us. The local Christians
were spreading the message themselves. Martin's training-class
for our church elders and deacons died a happy natural death.
Those who used to come found themselves so involved in evangelism and Bible teaching that they had no time to attend any
more.

A lad in his early twenties lived and worked in the church
office opposite. Si Dalan was badly maimed in one foot. He
would limp over to our house when his day's work was finished,
and chat and keep us informed of local gossip.

'Make yourself at home,' we had said to him very early on. 'Just feel as though this were your own house.'

'I'd better not do that,' he replied laughing, 'or I could help myself to anything I pleased . . . and that smart umbrella rather tickles my fancy,' he added, experimenting with opening and closing it. We had not then learnt the Karo custom about family ownership.

Si Dalan had taken it upon himself to run a Sunday School in the village of Semangat some distance away. Semangat means 'energy' or 'vitality'. The church there was the very opposite of this. When he first started, only a dozen children came and the church service which followed was attended by five or six women at best. But Si Dalan had a gift for telling stories, and tucked into the exciting details he could get a good deal of teaching across. Music was another of his strong points. He was the one to whom we turned for help with translation of new hymns, and when we left I gave him my piano accordion.

Under Si Dalan's faithful care and colourful gifts the church in Semangat grew. Six months later we went with him again one Sunday. It meant catching a seven a.m. bus (which probably would not leave eventually until after eight a.m.) and a three-quarters-of-an-hour walk along a cart track. Si Dalan's halting limp made the going even slower, but we admired his pluckiness as he determinedly dragged his crippled foot along.

To our surprise the Sunday School had grown to fifty children and a proper church service was now being held, with an elder in charge. Eagerly they bought up our Christian books and seemed keen for more. Semangat was at last beginning to live up to its name, and under God this was all due to a crippled lad.

A terrific rainstorm broke as we left for home, and we raced for shelter to a small thatched hut on the edge of the fields. The high winds drove the rain along almost horizontally, so that the tiny roof was quite inadequate. Our coveted black umbrella offered some protection! After nearly an hour huddled together, with all of us soaking wet, the rain eased off and we were able to pick our way along the muddy track to where we could catch a bus. Standing at the cross-roads Martin pointed out a small house to me. 'The snake elder lives there,' he said. 'Do you remember me telling you about him? He catches snakes with his bare hands and cuts them up for medicine. His house is decorated with snake-skins of every kind. There's one long skin which goes all the way up one side of his cupboard and down the other. He told me he's not a bit scared: "An agile man is always faster than a snake," he said. Still, I'd rather him than me.'

Eventually a bus rattled towards us. As usual it was crowded beyond capacity. People were hanging on at the back and sides, and a couple were sitting on the roof. Somehow room was made for us to squeeze in. Wet, tired, but feeling it had been so worthwhile, we at last arrived back home. It thrilled us to see what God was doing through the local Christians.

Another letter home from Martin about this time read:

Yesterday I went to a 'kampung' where I had never visited the church before. There is a new young Bible teacher there — one of the twenty I used to teach in Medan! It is a tiny congregation and not very alive, so he has a big job to do there with no help from anyone! He preaches two to three Sundays a month, leads the weekly Bible Study and Sunday School. He also teaches twenty-four hours of Bible a week in the primary school. For this work he gets enough rice to live on, together with any gifts or vegetables people like to give him. Plus that he gets 3/6d a month — a haircut alone costs 1/9d! But he is happy there and seems to be throwing himself into the work which God has given him — and no complaints.

A year later when we revisited this church a congregation of two hundred and fifty adults were present! God had blessed the sacrificial work of this young man straight from Bible School.

Amusingly, Martin's letter had continued with a description of the vegetable-lorry on which he hitched a ride home:

The driver's horn was in some way connected to his gears, for whenever we began to go uphill and he changed down, the horn began to sound and could not be turned off in spite of all his efforts. But when we got to the top and changed up again the horn went off and all was peaceful! Very odd!

Life was certainly never dull in Karoland.

Between us we had travelled by almost every conceivable mode of transport. But Martin's worst experience came a short time later. We had both been back to the Nommensen Theological Seminary in Siantar, where Martin gave a detailed talk to a packed lecture-room on 'The Christian's Attitude to Communism'. The free flow of questions afterwards showed how topical this subject was. Then followed a few days in Medan, speaking at a Methodist Chinese Youth Conference. We spoke English with Mr. and Mrs. Baker, our kindly hosts, and Indonesian with the Chinese young people. The Bakers were fluent in Chinese and knew no Indonesian, and the Chinese knew no English; so conversation was rather complicated.

On the Saturday morning we made the long bus journey back up to the plateau, to Kabanjahe. Martin ate a hurried lunch, unpacked and repacked, and then set off by himself for Laubalang. Laubalang lay in a remote part of Karoland we had never visited. The bus churned on for four bumpy hours across to the distant edge of our plateau and down the other side. Magnificent views of purple-clad mountain ranges stretched as far as the eye could see. The descent led into a steamy, hot plain riddled with mosquitoes. Martin was relieved to see that the houses where he was staying had mosquito nets above the beds. But after a late meeting, as he crawled wearily in to share his host's bed, he was greeted by an ominous buzzing. The nets had been left wide open all day instead of being carefully closed. They now harboured dozens of these tiny irritating creatures. Needless to say the night was a restless one, but at least it was bearable, as in the heat he had no asthma.

Life began again at five-thirty the next morning with a visit to the local stream for a wash, followed by a very peppery breakfast at seven a.m. Martin preached and led the eight-thirty service and by ten o'clock strolled with some of the church members to a coffee-shop on the road to wait for a bus home. They drank the usual glass of hot tea and waited. Hours went by and nothing came. The heat of midday mounted to a pitch, but no one offered Martin any lunch. The sun passed its zenith and slowly moved on. Still no sign of transport. Finally, about seven p.m. when there was still no bus, car or lorry of any sort, some food was brought.

They were just giving up at ten-fifteen p.m., having waited over twelve hours, when a solitary lorry appeared round the corner. The covered-in back was stacked high with large cylindrical baskets from which issued the unmistakable grunts and squeals of pigs. The animals had already travelled three or four hours and were covered in filth and dirt. The stench was overpowering when Martin looked inside. But there was nothing else for it. Together with a few other passengers he climbed on to the stinking, squealing heap of baskets. The pile was too high to allow him to sit up and there was no room to lie down. The large stalk of bananas he had been given as a 'thank-you' present stuck into his ribs, and the bunch of coconuts accompanying them thumped against his legs. Then the door slammed shut, plunging them all into darkness. The lorry lurched forward to the sound of the agonised shrieks of suffering pigs. The four-hour return trip was a nightmare. The 'road' was really only a stony cart track. Any specially big jolt brought further high-pitched squeals from the pigs — and a silent 'Hear! Hear!' from Martin. The only fact for which he could be thankful was that the law of gravity ensured that the pigs' filth travelled downwards! However, the powers of smell had no such limitations, and in the stuffy atmosphere they steadily increased.

Eventually he arrived home at three-fifteen a.m., having been dumped by the pig-lorry at the far side of the town, and so he had been forced to lug the heavy bananas and coconuts the half-mile home. There were times when we wished our Karo friends were not quite so generous! Our water shortage and living conditions prohibited the hot cleansing bath he would so dearly have loved. But he stripped off everything and washed

177

as best he could in a kettle full of warm water, while I made him a hot drink.

Several people asked us why we did not buy a car. It would certainly have made a tremendous difference, saving us hours of travel and much wasted energy, and we had the money for it if we wished. But would it have been right to set ourselves above our Karo colleagues? Only the very wealthy one or two owned their own cars. A few others had the use of a jeep for their work, but everyone else travelled by bicycle or public transport. We were fighting down an image of bygone days where the white man lived in style and the locals had little. We were convinced that as far as possible we should limit ourselves to the way they lived. Even so, our good strong cycles, bought in Singapore, were the envy of some. Nothing of this quality could be bought locally.

This determination of ours applied not only to transport but also to many other matters. We lived in a home just like one of theirs. I marketed, cooked and washed without hiring a servant until our first child was born. We refrained from photographing the many colourful people and scenes around us for a long time, because to own a camera appeared far too 'flashy'. If we had wished, we too could have bought 200 watts of electricity for a high price as soon as we arrived, and have saved much trouble fussing with paraffin lamps. But all this was well worth-while. The Karos took us into their hearts and homes as one of themselves. Confidences were shared, sorrows unburdened and problems talked over in a way which never would have been possible if we had set ourselves on a pedestal of material things.

But of course there were frustrations. The best way to cope with these was to develop a sense of humour. Take the post. One day the postman cycled past our house. He waved to me cheerily as I stood in the doorway. 'There are too many letters for you,' he called out. 'I couldn't manage them!' I felt the indignation rise as I watched him continue round the corner. 'The cheek of it! What was he paid for if he couldn't even bring our letters! The only thing to do was to pray for the grace of God, and later on, when I had time, turn up smilingly at the post office and ask politely for our letters, as if this were what happened every day.

All our time in Sumatra the postal system was chaotic. For months at a time there were no air-letter forms to buy, so we had to send our weekly letters home in an envelope, which was far more expensive. We ordered the air-letter forms eventually from Jakarta but it took them two months to arrive. A cable from Singapore on March 3rd telling us that an expected guest would not be coming was presented to us six weeks later! In the meantime Martin had travelled all the way down to Medan and out to the airport, making arrangements to carry her luggage — and so wasted a whole day as she never turned up. Our Christmas cards and calendars, posted well within the international dates specified, began dribbling in to us around March and April. However, it helped to spread the enjoyment out, and it was nice to know someone was remembering us — even if the thought had first started on its way to us six months before!

Often air-letters from England came sooner than a letter from our Mission headquarters in Singapore or Jakarta. Our literature orders from Jakarta took two to three months to arrive, which made it almost impossible to know how many of each sort of book to order. The amusing procedure of gaining possession of these parcels could be frustrating too.

Periodically in among our letters we would find a slip of paper which read: 'The following parcels numbered ... have arrived at the post-office for you, please go and collect them.' Thirty to forty parcels were indicated. Armed with this sheet of paper, Martin would hopefully turn up at our local post office. Having patiently waited his turn he produced the slip. 'Parcels!' was the comment. 'I can't see to them yet. Wait there!' Every other customer was served first and finally, when a protracted lull in business came, the clerk turned to Martin, 'Step behind the counter, sir.'

There lay a great pile of parcels which had now to be laid out in neat rows according to their numbers and matched carefully with the numbers on Martin's slip.

'783,592 ... 783,593 ... 783,595 ... where's 594?' came the anxious query. Together they hunted high and low for it — unsuccessfully. Martin pointed out that there was no evidence there ever was a 594. 'Didn't you write the numbers on, yourself?' he asked, 'and then make out this slip from those numbers?'

'No, it was the other man — he's gone to lunch!' retorted the clerk sharply. (It was still only ten-thirty a.m. — one hour already had passed at the post office — but Martin made no comment on the 'lunch'.)

'Well, what can we do? 594 obviously isn't here!'

'We'll fill out this form in triplicate, asking permission to tear up your slip. Here — you fill in the details,' said the harassed clerk and with a sigh of relief turned to another customer.

The 'forms in triplicate' had then to be signed by the Head of the post office and the Deputy Head. One was not at work that day. 'He's gone to his grandmother's funeral, you know,' said the clerk confidentially, warming up a little now that he felt he knew how to deal with officialdom.

'Please ask the Deputy to sign then,' requested Martin.

'Oh, they *must* sign simultaneously,' replied the shocked clerk. 'Come back tomorrow and we'll see to it then!'

Tomorrow Martin was lucky if he obtained the required signatures. It would probably be at least 'the day after'. And then he must work with speed. With luck he could fill out the new slip with all the numbers (taking great care to omit the offending 594) and get the double signatures on the bottom before either the boss or his deputy left early for his niece's wedding.

Finally came the moment when all those thirty to forty parcels became Martin's own possession. But how was he to get them home? The clerk was obviously nervous at having 'cleared' parcels lying on the counter. Martin sped home on his bike. 'Quick Elizabeth, call Rachel and Rasmita and anyone else you can find. We must get the parcels home.'

'My scones will be ruined,' I groaned as I brushed the flour off my hands. But we all raced back. The Indonesian girls piled their heads high with half a dozen of the flatter parcels. Martin and I attached as many as possible to our cycles, slipping the string on to the brake-grips and the lamp-brackets. Others were tied on to the carrier. The fingers of our left hand were slipped through the strings of four or five others, and finally we managed to stagger home with the lot.

The crowning incident came one day when we were told to collect a solitary parcel from England. When we arrived at the post office, the official informed us that he was charging us for storing it for us! We asked him in future not to bother to store parcels or letters — just to deliver them without delay!

But the warmth of our Karo friends' love and generosity far outweighed any inconvenience due to red-tape. And when President Suharto came to power in 1965 he not only battled with corruption but also attempted to combat bureaucracy and inefficiency at all levels.

Our Annual Indonesian Field Conference for all O.M.F. workers in that country was due in August. We looked forward to a break, and planned to combine it with a much-needed holiday in Singapore. Unfortunately, the price of air tickets to Jakarta suddenly rose sharply and made that part of the trip impossible. The agent told us it had risen by 300 per cent, and proceeded patiently to explain the mathematics involved. 'They used to cost 8,000 rupiahs. A 300 per cent rise equals 24,000 rupiahs. Add the original 8,000 rupiahs and the present cost is 32,000.' It was slightly bewildering, but whether it boiled down to 24,000 or 32,000 rupiahs, it was still too expensive.

We planned, therefore, just to go across the water to Singapore and Penang. Our routine cholera injections had to be seen to. Mine went smoothly. But the nurse put Martin's in far too low down. It must have hit a nerve as he felt a shooting pain down his arm, and passed out. When he came round he had lost the use of his arm. However, no one except us appeared too perturbed. He managed as best he could, and after a few days was gradually able to use the arm again.

A request was sent to our headquarters in Singapore to purchase our holiday air-tickets and post them to us without delay. Because of the exchange rate, we should have paid two or three times as much if we had bought them locally. Time passed and

181

no tickets appeared. With two weeks to go before our holiday, Martin made the long trip down to Medan to visit the central post office. Perhaps he might be able to locate the letter there. It was no good hurrying things, so he spent half-an-hour chatting with the junior official in charge of overseas mail before getting down to business.

'Well . . . you can have a look if you like,' the man finally agreed, when Martin explained why he had come. 'But I don't suppose you'll find it.'

He led the way into a warehouse, filled with a jumble of parcels. A narrow gangway ran down the centre. Loose piles indicated various areas of Sumatra. But chaos reigned. Parcels were hurled by a couple of sorters right across the room. One bounced off a table some fifteen yards from the throwers and skimmed past Martin's head. The official waved vaguely in the direction of another pile, and said those were for Karoland. But it was like looking for a needle in a haystack. After a short, fruitless search Martin gave up. The head of the post office assured him that letters from Singapore were guaranteed to arrive in Kabanjahe in three days. When Martin remarked that this was not his experience, the official finally agreed that this was in reality just the theory. The practice of it was not in his hands! But they were all very friendly and one dared not take offence.

However, the Saturday before we were due to leave, the tickets arrived at Kabanjahe post office, so maybe Martin's visit had not been in vain after all, but the post office did not normally deal with registered letters on a Saturday. Then, on opening the envelope we found the tickets were for the wrong airline. The planes for this other line left on different days. We would now have to leave a day early. First thing on Monday morning I went down to Medan to make our booking with the other airline, while Martin closed house and took the regular meetings, and then raced after me early on Tuesday.

Thankfully, we sank into the comfortable seats of the plane that afternoon. Our first seventeen months in Karoland had been momentous ones, and we were now looking forward to a good holiday before returning to our work in Karoland again.

'I had such an encouraging visitor, just before I came away,' Martin remarked, as the plane started to taxi down the runway. 'He was a little old man. I don't remember meeting him before, but he was so friendly and open. We talked about Christian things together, and he said, "It's as though all my life I've been climbing a tree, but I hadn't realised there was no fruit on it. Now I want to climb the Christian tree. If I get a few scratches it does not matter, as I know I'll find some fruit." '

Chapter Fourteen

God can be trusted

SOMEONE ASKED US recently, 'can you tell us of any big mistake you made in Sumatra, anything which if you had your time over again you would not have done?'

Martin hesitated for a long time and then thoughtfully replied, 'There are two things which I could call major mistakes; and yet, looking back, in the goodness of God, He overruled them both for good.'

The first mistake was overwork. The second I shall describe later. Within a few months of our arrival in Kabanjahe opportunities for work began to snowball. A year later there was such a hunger for Jesus Christ, such open doors to preach Him, that we felt we could have placed ten missionary couples and still have had more than enough for each one to do. It was no wonder that our programme was full — and no wonder that our health began to fail. We tried to keep a 'Sabbath' day, midweek of course, but it was difficult to relax. If we stayed at home, visitors would come. If we went out, 'Where are you going?' we were asked, and a reply of 'Just for a walk' brought looks of blank incredulity.

Martin's asthma dogged him the whole of our two years in Kabanjahe. Three times I had to call someone to him in the middle of the night; and oh, the agony of watching an inexperienced male nurse jabbing at his arm again and again in order to give an intravenous theophiline injection! I was perpetually succumbing to colds and sore throats, and after Andrew's birth had a succession of boils. On our next brief holiday in Prapat my boils were so bad that I could neither swim nor walk, and wondered why I had ever bothered to come all this way.

And yet in the light of the fact that the Lord was moving us on to something else, we are glad that we overworked. Those early days when opportunities were beginning to snowball were crucial. Under God's hand we are glad that we seized them to the full.

I remembered the Vice-Principal of my Bible college telling us, 'God doesn't expect you to burn *out* but to burn *on*.' Yet there are times when he asks us to give every ounce of our strength to an opportunity which may never come again.

Paul describes his great ambition as '*Now* as always Christ shall be magnified in my body, whether by life or by death.' Alec Motyer in his book *The Riches of Christ* comments on this verse: 'How these words "now as always" need to eat their way into heart and mind and conscience alike! For all of us each passing moment is a unique thing, unlike anything else, unrepeatable. It is now, now, now, that we must show how great Christ is. Never again will we have the chance to live for Him through *this* moment; never again will we have the chance to please Him in *this* circumstance; never again will He be gladdened by the trust in Him which we have shown in the face of *this* test.'

After only two years of serving God in Indonesia the opportunity has not been given to us again. Martin and I are glad that we spent all we had for Christ when we could.

Before I describe our other mistake I want to tell of another wonderful time when God showed His power in direct answer to prayer. As a child in far-off China, I had seen God work for people. I had known that other people staked everything on the God who is real, and found Him to be utterly reliable. Now, as a grown woman, a wife and a mother, I had many opportunities of knowing for myself the constant loving faithfulness of my Father in Heaven.

Christmas 1963 had come and gone. The rainy season was over. It was now mid-February 1964. Hot bright days followed each other, with high winds which blew the dry dust of the road over everything. Everything felt gritty to the touch. Martin's desk under the window had to be dusted two or three times a day.

It was six a.m. one morning, and I was just finishing dressing. 'No water's coming through!' announced Martin glumly, returning with two empty buckets.

'Why not?' I wanted to know. 'What's the matter?'

'When the Dutch left there were two pumps. When one stopped working, no one bothered to mend it: the other one was O.K. Now that's gone bust!'

'How long will it be before it's fixed?'

'No one knows. Sibekal, down the road, says they'll probably have to send to Jakarta for new parts. He generally seems to know. But that will take months!'

'We can't live for months without water,' I replied incredulously. 'Someone will have to do something about it.'

But 'someone' never did! Our town of over 20,000 people found itself suddenly without a water supply.

Rachel and Rasmita set off with a bucket each to the pump-house. It was situated in a deep hollow, a mile out of town. A long flight of steps, cut in the bare earth, led to the small pond and little brick building at the bottom. Here a stream of people jostled one another up and down the steps in their effort to obtain some water. Two hours later the girls returned with one and a half buckets of water between them. Rasmita had slipped on the way up, as the steps were by now splashed and muddy. She was limping from a sprained ankle.

'Can't we get some water from the river?' I asked Rachel anxiously, as I helped to bind Rasmita's ankle.

'It's no use. I met Mother of Pesta on the way back. It's so crowded there you can't get near the water. And you know how steep a gorge it is.'

'Thank goodness we bought that large petrol drum,' I said to Martin. 'Maybe you could find one of our friends who owns a lorry and get him to fill up the drum with water from somewhere.'

Only the week before we had bought a forty-gallon petrol drum for water-storage. It had taken some of my precious detergent and several buckets of water to get it clean. Now it was standing empty in our back yard. We had intended to buy one for a long time, but somehow had only just got round to it.

187

Martin went out to find someone with a lorry and after a while came back. 'Piun says he'll be around about two o'clock. He was going anyway, to get some water for himself. And he'll take the Revd. Bukit's drum too.'

My sigh of relief was turned into a gasp of despair when Piun returned long after dark. All the nearby water-places were too crowded, so he had gone a long distance to a river. Our clean drum was filled with muddy river water in which leaves and twigs swirled around. However, there was nothing better to be had. I silently thanked God that at least we had bought the drum and cleaned it before this emergency arose. Having removed as many of the floating objects as possible we strained the water through one of Andrew's muslin nappies. Even though we boiled it for ten minutes to make it safe it still remained a dreadful colour. I vowed inwardly not to give any to Andrew. If he grew thirsty he would just have to have an extra feed from me.

Days passed; there was still no hope of the pump being mended. Michael's Karo home had a well in the garden, so he was all right; but I needed so much water to wash Andrew's nappies and to keep him clean that we began to get anxious.

'If the situation doesn't improve, Elizabeth, I think you ought to take Andrew down to Sybil's in Medan,' Martin announced at breakfast one day. 'I can beg a bit of water from Michael's house, but you need such an awful lot.'

We agreed that if nothing happened within the next two days, I would have to go. Together with Michael we prayed it over. If God wished me to stay He would have a way out of our difficulty. It would be heavy on Martin if I left him to do all the housekeeping as well as his teaching programme; but the Lord knew about that too. If He wanted me to go He would give Martin the extra strength.

That day passed and nothing happened. The next morning came and I was nearly at the end of our river-water after washing the nappies. Martin came in to lunch following a heavy morning's teaching. 'It looks like rain,' he said, putting his bike away just inside the front door.

'It can't rain. It's the dry season!' I expostulated, going over

188

to the door to have a look. 'Still, it does seem to be getting dark.'

'Here, let's hurry up with lunch in case it does!'

Sure enough, the skies grew black and the wind changed into a gale whipping the trees mercilessly and sending rubbish hurtling past our doorway. Before we had time to finish our meal the heaviest tropical storm we had ever seen burst upon us. Cracks of forked lightning split the sky, crashes of thunder rolled continuously overhead, and great heavy drops of rain began to spatter down. They gathered speed and changed into a torrent, crashing on to our tin roof with such a noise we could not hear ourselves speak. Laughing and shouting we joined the neighbours outside and watched the dry road fill up with puddles and the heavy rain wash everything clean. All the dirty water was tossed out of the bottom of the drum and it was filled to the brim with delicious clean rain water. As we splashed back and forth with our overflowing buckets, our kitchen water-butt was gradually filled too.

I glanced at my watch. Time for Andrew's two o'clock feed! He was normally awake by now and ravenously hungry.

'O God,' I prayed, 'please don't let him wake up just yet. I do want to catch as much water as possible before the rain stops.' Miraculously, in spite of the deafening peals of thunder and the torrential rain, he slept peacefully on.

'What else shall we fill?' called Martin, with another overflowing bucket in his hand. 'The butt and the drum can't hold any more.'

'Fill up the saucepans and the kettle,' I called over my shoulder as I hurried out with my empty bucket. 'The washing-up bowl could hold some too.'

Every conceivable container in the house was brought out, even the tin linings of our boxes! And as the rain gradually subsided we collapsed into helpless laughter at the sight of the kitchen floor, covered with containers of water of every size, shape and description. Yes, we could laugh. Our God had done it again.

Next day was market-day, and as usual many friends from outlying *kampungs* came to visit.

189

'Wasn't it wonderful to get all that rain yesterday!' we exclaimed.

'Rain? We had no rain. We saw the black clouds and the lightning, but no rain fell on us.'

As we talked with one after another it slowly dawned on us that, outside of the town of Kabanjahe, not a drop of rain had fallen. God knew exactly where it was needed.

This ample supply of water lasted us until the pump was finally mended.

Our other mistake was about Communism. Martin had made a special study of Russian political thought while at Oxford. He saw the growing influence of Communism in Indonesia and felt that the churches were not sufficiently aware of the Communists' basic atheistic attitude. At the Theological Seminary in Siantar his lecture on 'The Christian attitude to Communism' had been well received. Now he decided to tackle the subject in his fortnightly training course in Tigabinanga.

It was a foolish mistake. If politics ever came up in a discussion, even with friends, we would normally say, 'We are ministers of religion and have nothing to do with politics.' Yet Martin felt the question of Communism was so important that the Karo Church ought to be faced with it. To make matters worse, unknown to us, one of the Tigabinanga Church elders was Deputy Chairman of the Communist Party in North Sumatra. As Martin explained Communism's anti-God position, this elder rose to his feet and stalked out of the class. He presumed Martin knew who he was, and he took the incident as a personal insult. Of course, if Martin had known, he would have delivered his teaching more tactfully, or maybe not at all.

The Deputy Chairman gathered the other members of the Communist party together and discussed what should be done. They sent a deputation to the Mayor, who forbade Martin to enter the Tigabinanga region again. Groups in the coffee-houses were stirred up against him, and legal proceedings threatened. They were well within their rights because by Indonesian law it is an offence to say anything insulting against an officially recognised body. And the Communist Party was just that.

Horror seized us as we gradually realised what a hornets' nest we had stirred up. Martin could be thrown into prison and held for trial, and as the case against him could be amply proved, his sentence might well be harsh. We were due to leave for furlough in England in two months' time. I could not possibly leave with Martin in prison. What should we do?

Of all our problems in Karoland this was the greatest we had faced. We might have felt better if we had not been in the wrong. But we knew we were at fault. Would God help us now? What right had we to presume on His loving care when we had made such a bad mistake?

The days and weeks which followed were some of the most soul-searching times we had ever experienced. All we could do was to throw ourselves on the mercy of God and ask that for Jesus' sake He would help us. News came that law proceedings were to commence against Martin very soon. All peace of heart left us and sleep became impossible.

We felt we had let Michael down. What sort of an example had we been to him as senior missionaries? We had also let the Mission down: Overseas Missionary Fellowship would have a bad name in Indonesia now. We had let the Karo church down: were we not their guests? If anyone had ever felt their tail between their legs it was us!

After constant anxiety and several sleepless nights, Martin opened his Bible. He was reading in the Psalms, and his eye fell on a verse which caused a glimmer of hope to penetrate his dejection. 'As the mountains are round about Jerusalem, so the Lord is round about His people for evermore.' He raised his eyes and gazed at the mighty peaks around us. Huge and jungle-covered, they sprawled into the distance, culminating in the great Sinabung volcano. Something of their strength and peace spoke to Martin. 'Yes, the Lord is like those mountains,' he whispered to himself; 'imperturbable, immovable, powerful . . . and He is here to protect me.'

Still, the news was bad. Meetings had been held in Tigabi-nanga to denounce us. Letters were posted to Medan to notify the officials there as to what had happened. But the sharp edge of our anxiety began to dissolve. The Lord was on our side, even if we failed Him. He was still in control.

Before Martin left England God had spoken to him from a verse in the Bible: 'If we are faithless, yet He remains faithful — for He cannot deny Himself' (II Tim. 2: 13). During these days we found out how true these words are. O the infinite mercy of God shown to us when we least deserve it!

Right to the very day we left Indonesia we were still afraid of Martin being put in prison. Again and again we were told that legal action had started. But still nothing happened. Martin went to Medan to obtain our exit visas, wondering if these would be refused, yet after the usual tedious visits he found they were granted.

A shadow hung over all our farewells, but our Kabanjahe friends would have none of it. 'You have friends in high places here,' they told us. 'They'll do all they can for you. And you were quite right to teach us about Communism.' In the light of the attempted *coup d'etat* by the Communists in October of the following year, perhaps they were right. God had overruled our actions for good, and great blessing came to the Tigabinanga church once Communism was exposed. The high school, which had been a centre for Communist activity, swung round so completely that nearly every pupil there professed to becoming a Christian. Of course there were numbers for whom this was not a personal commitment, but it produced a complete change of climate for Christianity in the area. At the time, though, we knew nothing of all this.

As our date of departure drew nearer it was encouraging to see the many visitors who came to say goodbye. The villages which we had helped to evangelise each held a farewell service. Gifts they could ill-afford were showered on us — beautifully carved *kris* knives, rich cloth laced with gold thread, handsome Javanese pewter fruit bowls and serving spoons. But the gift which moved us most was given at Lingga. One of the 'ex-queens' stepped forward, her little old back bowed from years of toil, her wrinkled face shrouded by the usual dark headdress. 'We have been thinking of your mothers,' she said in a quavering voice, 'how kind they were to spare you to come so far. We

192

want you to take these as a present to them — as our thank you.'

She handed us two simple betel-nut bags such as every woman in Karoland owned. A gift from women, to women, to show they loved and appreciated the sacrifice.

Our eyes were misty as we took the little bags in our hands.

We set a date to leave Kabanjahe, all the time wondering if we would be summonsed. Then an added problem arose: how to cross over to Singapore. Since Confrontation all communication had long since been stopped between the two countries and even direct air flights were impossible now. As Martin discussed with the travel agent how we could catch our ship in Singapore towards the end of April, the clerk came up with only one solution. The nearest country with which Indonesia had any dealings was Thailand. There were no direct flights from Medan to Bangkok. The only possible way would be to fly nine hundred miles south-east to Jakarta, fifteen hundred miles almost due north to Bangkok and then nine hundred miles almost due south to Singapore: a total of three thousand, three hundred miles. It would involve gigantic expense, and was especially galling as Singapore was only five hundred miles away across the water!

Our good friend, the head of Goodyear Rubber for all North Sumatra, was also trying to leave for Singapore at that time. In spite of all his official contacts he was forced to take this circuitous route.

'It's all very well for him,' we commented. 'Goodyear will pay. But the Overseas Missionary Fellowship isn't rolling in money. Every penny that comes in has been sacrificially given. Still, if God wants us to do that, He owns even more money than Goodyear. He can provide it.'

At the beginning of April we moved to Medan, feeling it would be easier there to contact offices. Kind Methodist friends put us up. We were still anxious about the Communist affair and wondering if a summons might come any day. Martin went to every travel and shipping agent he could find in the city, and eventually came back with two possibilities. There were a few ships which still plied between Indonesia and Malaysia, even though the Government did not approve. Two were due within the next few days, and their agents had promised to keep in touch.

But a day or two later things looked hopeless again. Hot and tired, Martin came in and flung himself into a chair in the shade.

'It's no good. They've both gone,' he groaned.

'Gone! What do you mean?' I gasped. 'The agents promised to let us know.'

'They couldn't help it,' he replied dejectedly. 'One was kept waiting outside the port for so long that they decided to cut Malaysia out and go straight on to Djibouti. The other came late one afternoon and left early next morning without letting the agents know.'

'So it looks as though we'll have to do the long air trip,' I replied.

'Well, I'll go down to the harbour myself tomorrow and have another look round. I don't suppose it will do any good, but you never know. I can't go there today. I'm finished. Could you get me a cold drink, please?'

The next morning was spent in a long fruitless search at the port of Belawan. Up and down long gangways, scrambling over piles of rope, hunting in large warehouses for the ship's master, Martin made endless enquiries — but it was all to no avail. At last, hot and tired, he sat down on a pile of boxes and wiped his perspiring face.

Some dock-workers looked over at him. It was certainly strange, seeing a white man sitting there. One of them smiled.

'What are you doing?' he called out.

'Looking for a ship to Malaysia,' replied Martin with a forced laugh. He strolled over to them and began to chat. They smiled warmly when he said he was a minister working in Ka-roland. 'I'm a Christian too — and a Batak,' said one. 'You ought to contact Tuan Manik,' he went on; 'that's his office over there.'

'Manik?' replied Martin. 'Then he's a Batak too?'

194

'O yes, and a Christian. He'll be delighted to meet you. Go and knock on the door. I think he's in.'

Tuan Manik turned out to be just the contact we needed — God's answer to our prayer. He was the sole agent for a Dutch shipping line which had just recommenced trade with Indonesia after the War of Independence so long ago. Their first-ever ship into Medan would be arriving the next day and then sailing direct across the water to Port Swettenham, Malaysia. Manik had sole right to authorise what cargo or passengers it carried from Belawan. And when he heard our predicament, he gave us his permission to go on board. The contact came so unexpectedly, and everything fitted in so perfectly, that we were staggered by it all.

Martin arrived back elated. 'Quick, pack everything. We're leaving first thing tomorrow. I've found a ship.'

Getting through Immigration at Belawan the following morning was a problem. We had to state the port of disembarkation.

'Just write Port Swettenham rather illegibly,' said the friendly clerk over the counter, who saw how badly his country's trade had been hit by Confrontation and had no sympathy for it. 'Perhaps they won't be able to read it.'

The customs official was another Batak Christian and helped us all he could, but our hearts were not fully at rest until we felt the good ship *Utrecht* pulling out from the quayside, and saw that there was no police-boat chasing us to take Martin back and put him in prison.

In every detail of the crossing we saw God's good hand upon us. The bill for two pounds which the *Utrecht* charged us was ludicrous, compared with the expense of the suggested long airflights. The captain could not have been kinder, and went out of his way to make us comfortable. He even put his own private launch at our disposal to land us and our goods at the other end.

The only momentary qualm came when we realised that we should need money for a porter to take our luggage through customs and out to find a taxi to Kuala Lumpur.

'I only managed to smuggle four Malay dollars with us into

Indonesia,' Martin whispered to me. 'You're not legally allowed to take any at all, but I thought we really ought to have something by us.'

The porter demanded ten dollars at first, but when he found we could speak Malay and that four dollars was literally all the money we had, he agreed to do it. The taxi fare from Port Swettenham to Kuala Lumpur could be paid at the other end. And so we found ourselves speeding along the smooth dual-carriageway to our lovely Mission Home in Kuala Lumpur, thanking God for bringing us safely across and knowing that we should be in good time to catch the ship home to England.

Chapter Fifteen

Twenty Years On

NEARLY TWENTY YEARS later I have been asked to add a postscript to bring our story up to date. Another whole kaleidoscope of events has passed, full of colour, warmth and pathos. So it seems best to pull out a few sample snapshots of various situations.

I was struggling along a bumpy footpath, winding between a maze of little houses in a small town in Malaysia. Propped up with a cushion, baby Margaret peered over the sides of her springless wheeled carrycot, chuckling at the unexpected jolts. But I was hot and flustered, because little Andrew, just toddling now, insisted on 'helping me push'. Manoeuvring round pot-holes left by the heavy monsoon rain was difficult work. And Andrew's legs were so short we seemed to crawl along at a snail's pace. Flushed with the tropical heat, my blouse soaked with perspiration, eventually we arrived at my Bible class pupil's door. Desperately trying to hang on to my inward calm, I attempted to hold a worthwhile conversation. But keeping two small children out of mischief demanded so much attention that I finally came away wondering why I had ever bothered to visit.

'What sort of a missionary am I now?' I moaned to myself on the way home. 'All I do is change nappies and listen to childish prattle! I'm useless!'

After the wonderful time of working alongside Martin in Sumatra it was hard to be tied down to two small children. We had hoped to return to Karoland, but the political situation made it impossible. So Martin was pastoring a small English-speaking church in south Malaysia until relations between

Indonesia and Britain improved.

God's power, however, was not limited by political upheavals. In fact at that moment, he was using a Communist-inspired *coup d'état* in Jakarta to bring about His own purposes. Just as the plan was about to be executed, the plot was exposed and miraculously overturned. The near-disaster shook the whole nation of Indonesia deeply, and flung open a wide door for the preaching of the Christian faith. Hundreds and then thousands of people were converted; so that, in our area of Karoland and throughout the country as a whole, from 1965 to 1968 the number of Christians trebled. Growth has continued steadily, although not quite so dramatically, ever since then. And some would estimate the number of Christians in Indonesia today to be almost a quarter of the population. Just yesterday I read an account of what has been happening in the Karo Batak church in 1983; over seven and a half thousand baptisms were reported in one locality.

And what was the Lord teaching me through my very different situation? One thing was that I should not consider it my 'right' to be out where everything was happening. God wants us to be faithful to Him in the humdrum everyday things of life. I was longing to *do* something for God. I feel now He was saying to me 'just *be*'. He had made the world with mothers and children, this was all part of His perfect plan, and I needed to learn to enjoy it – enjoy being a mother, enjoy my children and above all enjoy my relationship with my heavenly Father in the role He had given me.

At the time it felt interminable. The children's ability to become independent grew so slowly! As I look back now I can see it was only a relatively short stage, though a very vital one. Psychiatrists have only comparatively recently become aware of the crucial part these early years play in a child's life. I did have a vital ministry, although I could not see it. My children's whole later development was being shaped in those days – their sense of security, their ability to relate to others, their moral and spiritual values.

I came to see as well how important it was that I should keep the home running smoothly and happily, so that Martin could be set free for his ever-widening ministry. Just at that time, a couple of key O.M.F. families we knew had to return to their homelands because the wife cracked under emotional tension. And I thought to myself, 'if only I can keep Martin here in Asia that would be a worthwhile ministry!'

He was very understanding of my situation and saw to it that I had a weekly opportunity for spiritual outreach. So each Saturday afternoon he played with the children while I taught a Bible class. They were a group of fourteen to fifteen-year-old youngsters, many of them facing intense opposition from their families because of their Christian faith and because it was seen as denying their own nationality and cultural inheritance.

Their problems were so acute that they prompted me later to write a book on it. I longed to share with Christians in England what tremendous tensions can be created by the decision to follow Christ when one comes from an Eastern religious background. So *Fear of Water* came into print. This was actually not the first book I had published through O.M.F. While on furlough our editor had written to me suggesting we put some of our experiences together, perhaps in the form of a children's book. I had no training in writing, and my first manuscript, *Batak Miracle*, needed a tremendous amount of working over and correcting. But this prodded me into attending writers' workshops and working on improving my style. And how marvellous it was that here was a ministry I could have while still remaining at home!

'It was awful!' they groaned, in answer to our question. The two young Chinese church leaders stepped inside our front door and sank onto the nearby rattan chairs. 'We did our best to be pleasant. We enquired after the pastor's wife and family. We asked how the Chinese-speaking congregation was doing, and expressed our gratitude for being allowed to use their church building. But we just didn't seem to be on the same wavelength.'

'The worst thing about the visit,' his friend cut in, 'was when he served drinks. He was really taunting us – teasing us – I have no other words to describe it! He produced hot

199

chocolate drinks all round, but then he never invited us to drink. We just had to sit there staring at it. And finally we had to leave without even tasting it! We feel so hurt, so degraded.'

Martin and I looked at each other. What could we say? We were all praying about improved relations with the Chinese-speaking congregation, and the visit of our two friends had been steeped in prayer. Their new pastor was an able, gifted young Chinese man, who had just completed a long theological training in the States. What had gone wrong?

A few days later we heard his side of the story. 'I don't understand your young people!' he exclaimed. 'I got my wife to make the best drink we have – not just cold fruit juice – but the most expensive milk and chocolate. And what do they but refuse to touch it? Walk out of the house without even tasting it! I've never been so insulted in all my life!'

It is this kind of episode that underlines the importance of understanding different cultures. The highly educated Chinese pastor, with his years spent in the States, thought that his young English-speaking guests would be quite westernised. There was therefore no need to ask them to drink. However, they were well aware of more traditional Chinese ways, and were anxious to be on their best behaviour. So they would not drink until invited. Both sides wanted to be courteous, but it actually led to a major misunderstanding.

It was to help our new missionaries begin to appreciate cultural differences that O.M.F. set up an Orientation Centre in Singapore. Being a fast-growing modern city, where English was used by many people, Singapore formed an ideal 'half-way house' between the western homelands and the scattered centres of missionary work throughout east Asia. Here the new missionaries could make a start on language study and begin their cultural adjustment in comparatively easy surroundings. Just as relationships between Indonesia and Britain were improving and we were wondering about the possibility of returning to Karoland, the Mission asked us if Martin would become Superintendent of the Orientation Centre.

We were very young for the job but it was something close to

200

our hearts, as we had experienced so vividly how differently other races can view a situation or express themselves. There were many practical details that could be passed on, such as how to eat neatly with one's fingers so as not to soil the hand, or manage a pair of chopsticks for a Chinese meal. There was need for an awareness of small details. For example, Malays pass a dish using the right hand only, whereas a polite Chinese uses both hands. But a deeper sensitivity was required in understanding other nations' thought forms and modes of expression.

One of our first group of new workers went to meet his English-speaking boys' class on his first Sunday in Singapore. 'How should I have dealt with the situation?' he asked us afterwards. 'I wanted to find out what they would like us to study together. Were there any special problems they were facing? Or anything that particularly interested them? But I couldn't get them to say. I did mention that I had jotted down a list of possibilities if they couldn't think of anything. But they wouldn't make any suggestions!'

We had to point out that, in Chinese eyes, to say you have already made a list is tantamount to saying politely that they must follow your ideas. They are far quicker than Britishers to pick up a hint, and would hesitate anyway to tell a 'teacher' what they ought to be studying.

We found that most new missionaries were psychologically prepared to adapt to Asian cultures, but many found it much harder to adjust to other westerners. Yet we were an international missionary society, and there needed to be appreciation of our own different backgrounds. There had to be a willingness to adjust to each other, and this was not always easy. The English folk resented occasionally being asked to break their boiled egg into a bowl and eat it the American way. And an Australian couple, being welcomed by Martin at the airport, had great difficulty in realising that he was not an affected snob when they heard his Oxford accent!

We were only thirty-three when asked to take on this responsibility and several times had new workers coming out who were senior to us in age. We must have made a number of mistakes, and were very conscious of learning on the job. I should have been much more aware of the needs of our domestic staff, and we were both lacking the wisdom and experience needed to counsel others. Working as we do now at a missionary training college we can see that God planned those two and a half years to highlight for us the problems of new missionaries and to help us begin to think through the best training procedures.

When the time for our second furlough approached, we had grown to love the work at the Orientation Centre and to feel more confident about our contribution to it. So it burst like a bombshell on us when one day we were called for an interview with the overseas director and informed that the Mission was not happy with our work. He wished to replace us with someone else. We felt this to be unjustified and came away feeling hurt and angry.

The more we dwelt on our soreness, the more self-justification and indignation grew. We felt misjudged, as though any success we might have had was being ignored.

Then I remembered with a start a verse my Bible College Principal had spoken on ten years before. Hebrew 12:15 warns against any root of bitterness being allowed to lodge in our lives. She had pointed out how bitterness can eat like a cancer into the heart. It starts often so small with the person feeling fully justified because of the extremity of the situation. But if allowed to take root it will gradually twist its clinging tendrils and smother any form of life.

So we faced our battle. And it was not easily won. Would we allow bitterness to take over?

The next morning the Lord spoke to me in an unmistakable way. I was reading Daily Light, and came across the words; 'The Lord has said to you, You shall never return that way again' (the title verse for February 4.) The words really hit me. Could it be *the Lord* who was saying to us that we were not to come back to this work at the Orientation Centre? I had thought it was merely the director! Twice more in the next few days came verses with the same thought. I am not usually guided by a 'verse from the Lord' taken out of context, but each time it happened I had that peculiar feeling that this was a special word from the Lord to me.

Yet here was my further struggle. Was not this a wrong decision made by our leaders? How could it be God's will? I knew that God could be trusted when we followed Him with full dedication. But what about *now*, when we felt a mistake was being made? Dared I believe that God could overrule this for good? That really was too much to ask! When we did God's will, of course He remained in control, but when our leaders apparently made a wrong decision, what then . . . ?

Gently and persistently as our last orientation course progressed the Lord called us to trust Him. The battle was not won in a day, and was harder for Martin as it clearly questioned his ability to handle people and lead a work of this calibre. Insecurities from his childhood reared their ugly heads. But very lovingly and firmly the Lord dealt with us. That final course with the new missionaries turned out to be the 'best ever', which did something to mollify the wound; and gradually God began to heal our bitterness.

We journeyed home to England wondering what God had in store for us next. The Mission leaders expected us to return to Indonesia. They invited us to visit Java to catch a glimpse of some of the strategic opportunities there. But Martin had no peace of heart that we were to work again in Indonesia. We travelled home the long way round the world in order to visit those of my family who were living in New Zealand and the States. Passing through America, both the O.M.F. offices, one on the west coast and the other on the east, asked Martin if he would join their staff. They realised his gift in speaking, and saw how valuable a contribution he would make in stimulating missionary interest and challenging young people to serve God overseas. We were attracted by the offer as America is such a land of opportunity, but were not entirely sure it was God's plan for us.

Starting on a deputation ministry in England, the U.K. Director soon made a similar suggestion to Martin. He would work on the home staff with opportunities to speak all over the country.

We felt baffled and somewhat bewildered at our inability to sort out God's guidance. It was not that doors were closed to us. On the contrary, so many doors were open and yet none seemed right. Guidance had seemed fairly straight-forward in the past. So what was wrong with us now? Were we being too subjective in relying on our feelings? Were we acting in some way that was preventing God from showing us what He wanted?

We prayed earnestly over each suggestion, and had to cast ourselves on God's grace in a new way. As our year's furlough came to an end, the Mission leaders kindly extended it for a further six months. We were still unclear which way to move forward, and Martin was having such a valuable speaking ministry they felt this was the best thing to do.

How beautifully God overrules the timing of events! We can now see that God could not have shown us the next step when we first started to pray about it, because the job was not even there! All Nations Christian College had not yet been formed. For some years three Bible Colleges (All Nations, Mount Hermon and Ridgelands) had been preparing to merge into one larger college, catering for both married and single students. Their aim was to provide a specialist course in cross-cultural communication. It was not to compete with other Bible colleges but to concentrate on preparation for missionary service.

With the merger now poised to take place, the board of governors was praying about the appointment of a new member of staff. They approached Martin. Everything seemed to fall into place as he thought about it; our growing interest in preparing people for missionary work; the glaring gaps he had become aware of in his own preparation; the thought he was giving to what should be included in missionary training; the way God had moved us from place to place during our time overseas, so that we had experience with many of the major religions of the world – Islam, Hinduism, Buddhism, Taoism, Confucianism, Sikhism and Animism; the opportunity we had enjoyed of working both in resistant areas and in a mass-movement situation. Here at last, he felt, was the way forward that God had been preparing for us!

However, I viewed the new proposition with reluctance. I had been called to be a missionary! I had no wish to stay on in England. Would I not be turning my back on God's call? I felt very upset at the prospect, and it took me some weeks before the Lord could show me what really was happening. I had been brought up in O.M.F. circles. All my life I had felt very close with the mission, and when I joined it felt to me like 'coming home'. Other people had talked about 'culture shock' going overseas, and I had never really understood them. On going back to Asia as an adult, it brought a thrill to me to be surrounded by Chinese sights and sounds and smells. Unwittingly, my missionary society had become my security.

Now the Lord was saying to me, 'Yes, I *did* call you. But that is not necessarily for a lifetime. Now I want you to move on. Can you trust me for your security when this large prop in your life is taken away?'

We were warned by a mature Christian friend not to take any rash steps. 'All Nations is a tiny, unknown college,' he told us. 'They are launching out on an enormous building project, with no financial backing. If it doesn't take off, in six months they will be bankrupt and your name will be linked to a fiasco.' Looking into the financial position we saw a new aspect of walking by faith. O.M.F., as a 'faith mission', relied completely on God touching people's hearts to supply their needs. As God sent in the money for a project, so they took this as His confirmation that they were to move forward. But All Nations was to go one step further; they were committing themselves in faith to the huge financial cost of new buildings *before* the money had come in.

After much prayer and heart-searching we both felt clearly that All Nations was indeed God's will for Martin. And as the months went by, the faith of David Morris, the Principal, was vindicated. The money for each successive bill came to hand just as it was needed.

Martin was soon absorbed in a busy college lecturing programme. David Morris had said to him, 'If you were planning missionary training from scratch, what would the course be like?'

There was a great sense of freedom and openness to the Lord. Between the various members of staff the course was shaped and re-shaped, constantly seeking for what were the key elements in training for cross-cultural communication. They were grateful not to be tied down to a rigid outside examination syllabus. But they also knew the importance of keeping academic standards high. The aim was to offer flexibility, with tailor-made courses. Each student would receive the training particularly appropriate to his own situation and future sphere of service. For this, David Morris introduced a tutorial system, and this was how I came to be involved in A.N.C.C. a few years later.

In the meantime I was experiencing the joy of ordinary family life in a settled home in England! I feel that this gave me emotionally an unpressured sense of well-being, what the Hebrews called *shalom*. And this was a necessary preliminary step before the Lord's wonderful gift to us of a third child, Ruth, after a seven-year gap.

Being linked with All Nations has widened our horizons dramatically. For some years we had prayed and worked for the spread of the gospel through S. E. Asia, enjoying its wealth of culture and history, peoples and beauty. But now we found that the whole world became our parish. Each year students come to us from twenty-five to thirty different countries, bringing amazingly different outlooks and a great variety of gifts. They are often involved in lectures and seminar discussions, so our western students are immediately grappling with the process of understanding other races. As they finish the course our students go to every corner of the globe, and enrich us with their reports and newsletters.

Gradually Martin's travelling ministry has developed further. First of all on the Continent, where he resurrected his rusty German after twenty years of disuse; and then much further afield. It is important in his work to keep abreast with what is happening in other parts of the world. Sharing with key national Christians and mission leaders is challenging and enriching.

One of the main lessons we feel we are learning at All Nations is pastoral care of others. As a staff team we are realising the importance of endorsing each other. With a group of strongly gifted individuals, from very varied backgrounds, it is easy to feel threatened by another's talents. But we need to express our appreciation of each other's unique contribution and accept our differences.

In tutoring the students we are learning to be unashamed of our own insecurities. We can meet them with an openness that is prepared to share weaknesses. None of us has had a perfect upbringing. All of us share the experience of hurts and bruises that have left their mark and limit our capacity for true wholeness in Christ. But as we come to understand ourselves more fully and to receive the healing that is there for us in Christ, we can help others open up to what God longs to do in their lives. This is a beautiful ingredient in the preparation of God's children for His service.

It is such a joy to be working at the College together! Many students have voiced their appreciation of the fact that we have 'husband and wife' teams on the staff. In these days when marriages are under so much pressure this can be particularly important. As a college we consider it vital that all wives are trained alongside their husbands. They are going to face demands overseas equal to any their husbands will grapple with. And they need to be prepared, both by a thorough grasp of the Christian faith and by a deep understanding of the religion and culture of the people to whom they are to minister.

Living a mile from college in a Hertfordshire village, we have felt a 'missionary' responsibility to our own community. Up to a year ago, the local Anglican church had only a tiny congregation, and the one 'Free Church' was almost on its last legs. We felt the most effective strategy was to follow Karo patterns of home-centred evangelism. I started a series of coffee mornings with various speakers who shared how the Lord Jesus makes a difference in ordinary life. From this we soon discovered who were spiritually open, and a ladies' Bible study group began. Realising that the men were not being reached, Martin began a similar meeting for them. They were planned as evangelistic Bible studies, so there was no need to be a Christian before coming. The main stipulation was that we wanted to see what the Bible had to say. Those in the group might not agree with it, or might not like its implications – that did not matter, it was up to them – but we were honestly attempting to find out what the Bible taught. We all took it in turns to offer hospitality so as to avoid any feeling of 'us' and 'them'. And everyone took their turn at leading, even if sometimes two people would do it together. It was exciting to hear of non-Christians who had spent three hours one week studying the passage in preparation for the meeting; and if they had to say they did not know the answer to a certain question, nobody minded.

It has been slow work, but over the years a steady stream of people have come to know Christ and been strengthened in their Christian faith. We often longed and prayed for a helpful church with which to link them; and now after twelve years the Lord has answered that prayer too. The church in the village is beginning to 'come alive'.

What of the future? Are Martin and I meant to stay on at All Nations indefinitely? Recently he received several offers of other work, one particularly that attracted him greatly. In fact last year Martin was saying to himself, 'Twelve years already at A.N.C.C. and now twelve years to go before retirement. Should I be looking elsewhere?'

We run a system of 'guidance clinics' at college for students who are unsure of their future. Two or three tutors will meet together with the students to discuss and to pray. Martin asked for one of these for himself, and it was very beautiful to be able to seek God's will together. Our own peace of heart echoed the unanimous agreement that we should stay on. Martin's job gives him the secure base and the intellectual stimulus he needs, and yet the wider challenge of travel and speaking. He is therefore required to practise what he teaches about adapting to other cultures. I have the joy of a happy home, three lovely children and a worthwhile but not too demanding part-time job.

Yet we need to be open to the call of God whenever it should

208

come to move on. It is so easy to cling to the security of the present position. However the future may work out, we are learning increasingly that *God can be trusted*.

Until the Day Breaks

The life and work of Lilias Trotter—pioneer missionary to Muslim North Africa

by Patricia St John

As a young woman who had just turned down the prospect of a brilliant career as an artist to serve Christ, Lilias Trotter's missionary call started as 'a strange, yearning love for those who were in the land of the shadow of death'. Despite being refused by a missionary society on health grounds, she was soon sailing into the port of Algiers to begin an evangelistic work that was totally unconventional for a European woman of the day.

The story of her 40 years of dedication to the task of building Christ's church in North Africa is told in this new biography by well-loved author Patricia St John, who herself worked for 27 years in the same area.

OM
publishing

Through Gates of Splendour

by Elisabeth Elliot

. . . Marg was standing with her head against the radio, her eyes closed. After a while she spoke: 'They found one body . . .'

Missionary history will never let us forget the five young American men savagely martyred by Auca Indians in the jungles of Ecuador as they attempted to reach them with the Word of God.

Elisabeth Elliot, widow of one of those men, records the story of their courage and devotion to Christ in the face of danger and difficulty.

The challenge of their expendability for God continues as strong today as it was at the time of their deaths in 1956.

OM
publishing

Shadow of the Almighty

by Elisabeth Elliot

'He is no fool, who gives what he cannot keep, to gain what he cannot lose'

So wrote Jim Elliot at the age of twenty-two.

'Seven years later,' writes his widow, 'he and four other young men . . . sat together on a strip of white sand on the Curaray River, deep in Ecuador's rain forest, waiting for the arrival of a group of men whom they loved, but had never met—savage Stone Age killers, men known to all the world now as Aucas.'

Here is the full story of the life and death of one of these five modern martyrs, compiled by his wife around the poignant and spiritual writings of his own journals.

OM
publishing